Drama and Diversity

For Morgan and Betsy:
The New Guard

"The self is not contained in any moment or any place, but it is only in the intersection of moment and place that the self might, for a moment, be seen vanishing through a door, which disappears at once."

—JEANETTE WINTERSON, *SEXING THE CHERRY*

Drama and Diversity

A PLURALISTIC PERSPECTIVE FOR EDUCATIONAL DRAMA

Sharon Grady

HEINEMANN
Portsmouth, NH

Heinemann

361 Hanover Street
Portsmouth, NH 03801–3912
www.heinemanndrama.com

Offices and agents throughout the world

The author and publisher wish to thank those who have generously given permission to reprint borrowed material:

Figure 3–1: "Hidden Rules Among Classes: A Quiz" from *Poverty: A Framework for Understanding and Working with Students and Adults from Poverty* by Ruby Payne. Copyright © 1995 by Ruby Payne. Reprinted by permission of the author.

Figure 3–2: Cover of *Fly Away Home* by Eve Bunting. Jacket copyright © 1991 by Ronald Himler. Reprinted by permission of Clarion Books/Houghton Mifflin Co. All rights reserved.

Figures 5–1 and 5–2: Stills from the video "It's Elementary: Talking About Gay Issues in School" used by permission of Women's Educational Media and producers Debra Chasnoff and Helen S. Cohen. Women's Educational Media, 2180 Bryant Street, Suite 203, San Francisco, California 94110.

Figure 5–3: Cover of *Asha's Mums* by Rosamund Elwin & Michele Paulse, illustrated by Dawn Lee. Published by Women's Press, Canada. Used by permission of the publisher.

Figures 6–1 and 6–2: Cover and illustration from *Oliver's High Five* written by Beverly Swerdlow Brown and illustrated by Margot J. Ott. Published by Health Press, Santa Fe, New Mexico. Used by permission of the publisher.

Library of Congress Cataloging-in-Publication Data
Grady, Sharon.
Drama and diversity: a pluralistic perspective for educational drama / Sharon Grady.
p. cm.
Includes bibliographical references and index.
ISBN 0-325-00262-2 (acid-free paper)
1. Drama in education. I. Title.
PN 317 .G65 2000
317.39'9—dc21

00-035058

Editor: Lisa A. Barnett
Production: Elizabeth Valway
Cover design: Jenny Jensen Greenleaf
Cover photo: "Liberty" actress—Krista Shafer in "Liberty!" by Chris Wells from COOTIE SHOTS: Theatrical Inoculations Against Bigotry, *created and produced by Fringe Benefits Theatre. Los Angeles premiere, October 1999.* COOTIE SHOTS: Theatrical Inoculations Against Bigotry *published by Theatre Communications Group, fall 2000. Costume designer: Martha Ferrara. Photo by Kathi Kent.*
Manufacturing: Louise Richardson

Printed in the United States of America on acid-free paper
Docutech EB 2009

Contents

Foreword

Sharon Grady "walks the talk." Unlike some White writers of theatre education texts—those who exploit and capitalize on the exploding market and demand for books on multicultural education and, in the process, misappropriate the canons of people of color, assume authority on multiethnic issues, and misrepresent in offensive ways the heritages and contemporary perspectives of those long silenced—Dr. Grady demonstrates a sensitive and well-researched grasp of today's complex social worlds in *Drama and Diversity.* In this book you'll be introduced to the theory and practice of classroom drama and theatre for youth from a *pluralistic* perspective—a perspective that acknowledges and respects the multiple lenses with which diverse people view the world and construct their identities.

This text is an important addition to the literature of drama with young people because it is so thoughtfully written, so much in harmony with contemporary thought and practice in education. Most impressive and groundbreaking in *Drama and Diversity* is its multidisciplinary integration of content. Grady has observed, as I have, the connections, collages, and overlap between and among such fields as drama education, theatre for youth, multicultural education, critical pedagogy, women's studies, anthropology, sociology, ethnography, cultural studies, and others. References to and insights from such writers as James A. Banks, Lisa Delpit, Peter McLaren, bell hooks, Clifford Geertz, and other key figures are essential contributions to the social issues she addresses, as well as testimony to the breadth of her scholarship. One indicator of an astute thinker is not just the answers she gives but the questions she raises. Dr. Grady has developed provocative yet pragmatic inquiries for readers under "Questions to Ponder," "Practical Problems to

Consider," and "A Case Study Situation" at the end of each chapter. These supplemental questions are just as insightful as answers, and are designed to evoke multiple perspectives and solutions during individual reflection and group discussion. Finally, *Drama and Diversity* is also a personal text. With unabashed honesty and refreshing vulnerability, Sharon Grady confesses her personal embarrassment and personal growth during epiphanies when her own cultural positions clashed with others. These autoethnographic stories are compelling, and illustrate how teachers must critically examine their own perspectives and assumptions of authority in the classroom.

In 1997, the *Hopwood v. State of Texas* ruling barred the law school at the University of Texas at Austin (my alma mater and Sharon Grady's institution) from using race or ethnicity as criteria for student admissions. As a consequence, minority applications and thus admissions declined, not only within the law school but across the entire university system as well. Personally alarmed by national news reports of an anti–affirmative action sentiment and racist statements by some of UT-Austin's establishment professors, I instituted a personal boycott of the university in support of my brothers and sisters of color. I wrote a letter to selected Department of Theatre and Dance faculty, and to departmental, college, and university administrative leaders informing them of my reactions and decision. It was carefully worded, though, to acknowledge that my colleagues at UT-Austin—including Sharon—were not the targets of my rage, as I wrote to her:

> I know that you . . . and others in the Department of Drama and Dance are not only supporters of the principles of affirmative action, but also advocates of human rights. My problem is not with you—it's with the larger system of minority oppression manifested in the Texas powers-that-be. . . . I will not return to UT-Austin, nor can I speak well of the school and its dismantled affirmative action policy, until I read that the sociopolitical climate and policies have changed for the better on your campus.

Responses I received from selected individuals at UT-Austin included what I interpreted as defensiveness ("If you had bothered to speak with one of us here we could have told you how this decision . . . "), denial ("It's not as racist as you think"), and resistance to honoring my feelings ("I am disappointed that you have chosen to react in such a simplistic way"). Oppressed people often feel silenced—not silent, but *silenced*. In my personal and professional interactions, I feel I have voice. The problem is that, sometimes, certain individuals I'm talking to aren't *listening*. To perceive me—a gay Hispanic—as "lesser than," and thus to dismiss my opinion, to misunderstand my perspective, to negate what I value, is to silence me. What good is voice if no one listens? Sometimes I feel I have to repeat what I say before I truly believe others are listening. Sometimes I feel I have to repeat what I say before I truly believe others are listening.

Sharon Grady was the only respondent to my letter who demonstrated an understanding of *my* perspective because she struggled to examine *her own* position within the Hopwood conflict. It is one of the most treasured pieces of correspondence I have ever received, and I quote various selections from that letter to illustrate her openness, her empathy, and her humanity:

> I respect your decision and admire your courage and conviction. Your letter has made me pause to reconsider and to carefully observe what is happening here in Texas and my own role and responsibility. The Hopwood decision has forced many of us to reassess how best to respond to the continuing inequities imbedded in higher education. The question is how to proceed. The sting of your [boycott], mixed with the realization of how students in my own community are viewing UT after the Hopwood decision, has led me to a new commitment to the outreach efforts needed by our university, and has encouraged me to more proactively find ways to begin dialogues concerning where we go from here to effect change.

My boycott of UT-Austin is now postponed because a Texas law, instituted after the Hopwood case, guarantees the top 10 percent of graduates from every Texas high school a spot at the public university of their choice. This action opened UT-Austin's doors to high schools with large percentages of students of color in an attempt to restore the campus's ethnic diversity to what it was under affirmative action; time will reveal how this plan unfolds. Nevertheless, amidst all the turmoil of those heated letters, one person listened, reflected, and acted. That's why I proclaim that Sharon Grady "walks the talk." So, in *Drama and Diversity*, follow where she takes you, and listen to what she has to say.

Johnny Saldaña
Arizona State University

Preface: A Dilemma

Let me start with a true confession. I once blew up my drama class. Granted, it was many years ago when I was just starting out, but I set up a drama about a group of offstage terrorists who had seized an airplane and when the "hostages" did not cooperate, I blew them up. Harsh, yes—and fairly embarrassing in retrospect—but *at the time* consistent with what I thought was "good" drama practice. By that I mean it had a plot that was gut-wrenchingly personal and "about us," yet it elicited strong emotional involvement with supposedly "universal" themes, and was motivated by vaguely archetypal heroes and villains. After all, as the flight attendant who unveiled the gravity of the situation as the drama progressed, I was merely acting on the orders of the evil, unseen, Middle Eastern "others" we had tacitly conjured.

During reflection on the drama, some of the college students I had experimented on actually cried and told me it was one of the most moving experiences they ever had. In particular, a letter the "hostages" had been asked to write to the one person they loved most (just in case they did not survive the ordeal) would be "treasured always." I should have been pleased about the level of engagement and the depth of the emotions mined. But instead, I was terribly unsettled. This drama had been little more than emotional manipulation on my part and turned into a kind of group therapy session, which certainly has its place, but not in a college classroom where I was working with preservice elementary teachers who were curious about how they could use improvisational drama with *their* students. Like many of them, I was much more interested in encouraging people to think instead of to cry. But what had I given them the opportunity to think about? Lurking beneath the emotion-laden surface of this drama were troubling assumptions about how "foreigners" threaten our happiness and way of life. What had I done!?

I mean, who *were* our captors, anyway? No one, including me, questioned the immediate assumption that these unseen villains *must* be ruthless "Arabs"—the generic Middle Eastern "others" of choice at that time of escalating tension in the Persian Gulf. It slowly dawned on me that the cost of *not* paying close attention to the stereotypes often generated in drama and theatre work is that our unchecked assumptions about cultural "others" often uphold prejudice and bias, even if that's not our intention. Further, as I began to question how my own sense of identity, privilege, and power was connected to this troubling representation of race, I wondered about the impact on my students. Were any of them from Middle Eastern descent? If so, how had I unwittingly denigrated their ethnic heritage or denied their potential or abilities? The casualties were endless.

I begin my meditation on drama and diversity with this dramatic dilemma as a way to point to the journey I embarked on twelve years ago after I conducted this drama. This journey has led me to question many things about my own practice and pedagogy, including:

- What informs the choices we make as we construct drama work?
- How do our choices open up areas of learning or close down areas of inquiry?
- What is the impact of our choices on students? What are we giving them the opportunity to ponder?

As I have grappled with these questions, I have returned again and again to two things that often motive our choices: our *ideological positions* (or what we think and believe) which are connected to, although not determined by, our complex *identity locations* (which include racial and ethnic background, social class position, gender, ability, sexual orientation, as well as other markers such as religious or political affiliations). Both profoundly affect how we construct our work and the areas of learning we give students the opportunity to explore. The tricky part, of course, is that our students are also grappling with similar complex combinations of identity markers and belief systems. The harsh reality is that our pedagogical and artistic choices may (and often do) unintentionally negate or clash with our students' experiences, realities, or beliefs. This unacknowledged or uncritical collision can close down student engagement and substantive learning and reinforce negative understandings of social processes. What do we do about the potential dissonance between our identity locations and beliefs and those of our students?

Developing a Pluralistic Perspective

Difference is a factor in any set of human relationships—whether acknowledged or not. In the U.S., demographic shifts have brought more attention to how difference plays out in classroom interactions, particularly between teachers and students. The past ten years have seen increased attention paid to multicultural education practices that acknowledge the need to attend to cultural difference in both course content and student interactions. In addition, predictions about future population demographics indicate that approximately 46 percent of students in the year 2020 will be students of color (Banks and Banks 1997, vii). These eventualities have sounded an important wake-up call. What do we need to know in order to serve *all* the young people we interact with now and in the future?

This is an especially crucial question when we consider the demographics of the field. For example, there is a good chance that most people who read this book will be White. This is consistent with findings by multicultural theorists Christine Sleeter and Carl Grant (1998), who point out that approximately 90 percent of people involved in education are White (89.6 percent in 1986, with the number of teachers of color steadily declining) (1). Following the statistics for the education profession, there is also a good chance that most readers will be, like me, middle- to upper-middle-class, able-bodied, heterosexual, and female. I do not bring this up as an exclusionary tactic (of course, there is diversity in our field) but rather to point to the fact that many of the young people we work with may not share *any* of our identity locations. How, then, do we effectively navigate between our assumptions about the world and theirs?

Now more than ever there is a need for a pluralistic perspective in our drama and theatre work. By this I mean a more in-depth understanding of and respect for the identity locations that mark us as different from one another. Specifically, from our power positions as teachers, drama leaders, and directors, we need to develop the ability to look beyond our own ways of viewing the world. Psychologist Susan Fiske (1993) believes that people in power stereotype because they don't feel they need to pay attention to other people's circumstances. How do we avoid falling into that category? How can we, instead, carefully analyze our interactions with culturally diverse students and refigure the kinds of cultural knowledge we pass on?

What does it take to have a pluralistic perspective? I believe it requires three things: 1) carefully analyzing various facets of identity and difference, 2) directly addressing these differences with young people as a way to build an ongoing understanding of diversity, and 3) adjusting our approach to teaching to ensure that we are creating environments and learning experiences in which all students have a place and voice. I believe that our understandings of specific identity categories or locators such as race and gender are socially constructed. By that I mean, they are *not* somehow inherent or biologically determined but instead come to be defined in relation to privilege, bias, and power. Although socially constructed, these identity categories have a profound impact on young people and their ability to achieve their full potential. For teachers and artists working in an art form that trades on the creative construction of "other" worlds, this book provides a challenge: how might we build an awareness of the constructedness of social categories in our classrooms and theatre work and encourage students to critically question these constructions? How might we actively mitigate against the effects of limiting understandings of difference by closely examining the ways in which we think about what we do as teachers and artists?

Subject of Drama/Drama Subjects

Some of us teach drama and theatre as a subject, some of us use drama as a learning tool, some create various kinds of performances *for* young people while some create plays *with* young people, and some of us do all of the above. I am not interested in revising old debates over which work has more value. Instead, I am interested in asking larger questions about the nature of pedagogy and practice. I am unashamedly advocating that a pluralistic perspective can help educational drama teachers and theatre practitioners to pointedly structure work in ways that help students reflect on issues related to identity and difference. But please do not misunderstand—I am not calling for a simplistic, uncritical or strictly humanist use of drama, so deservingly critiqued by David Hornbrook (1992, 1998). Rather, I am suggesting the strategic use of critical analysis in our work to help more rigorously examine how bias operates, how privilege works, and how stereotypes wound. This is in contrast to "reflection" that is focused exclusively on self-referential feeling or vague notions of universality. I am simply advocating a shift in how we think about drama work as we do it, as we critique it, and as we extrapolate on what our fictional work has to do with the broader context of the "real" world(s) we inhabit.

Not unlike my British colleague Helen Nicholson, I am not advocating the use of drama to evangelize on behalf of multicultural education in general or as activism in support of any one identity location. Rather, I am interested in how a critical awareness of bias, stereotyping, prejudice, and normalized assumptions about "the way it is" can encourage students to, as Nicholson (1995) says, "produce interesting, challenging and increasingly sophisticated work" (35). This kind of sophistication can result in work that goes beyond merely reflecting reality, striving instead, as Nicholson points out, to rewrite it (36). Whatever we teach, our work is loaded with our assumptions about how we see the world. How do we take responsibility for these assumptions? For me, it's a pedagogical concern tied to how we view knowledge and our place in its construction.

Drama and Identity: Moments of Pluralistic Practice

Consider the following dramatic moments:

A drama workshop run by Johnny Saldaña invites students to think about discrimination in a unique way:

> A group of upper elementary children are considering what they would do if they were told they could not participate in a game because of their skin color. In small groups, the person whose name is first in the alphabet is designated as the "purple person." This person will "try on" what it feels like to be discriminated against by the group. An interesting scene develops:
>
> PURPLE CHILD: Why can't I play with you?
> FIRST CHILD: Because we don't like purple people.
> SECOND CHILD: Yeah, go away.
> PURPLE CHILD: Well, if you're the kind of kids that don't like purple people, I don't wanna play with you.
> FIRST CHILD: That's fine with us! (Purple child walks away.)
> TEACHER: Wait a minute, what do you mean, you "don't wanna play" with us? What's wrong with us?
> FIRST CHILD: Yeah!
>
> The teacher subsequently uses the situation to discuss the nature of prejudice and possible strategies to help combat it. (Saldaña 1999a)

In a school auditorium in Los Angeles, a lively scene from *Cootie Shots*, a series of playlets about diversity, begins to unfold:

> The audience hears a sea of voices calling out names that elementary school age children use to put each other down. Tonia, a fifth grader, enters the playing space: "Have you ever been called a name that wasn't very nice? Something really awful and mean? I have. It's not even anything about me, really, but it still hurts real bad. I mean, it doesn't even have anything to do with me. Well, it kinda does. (Pause.) My name's Antonia and my brother, Alphonso, is gay. Being gay means that he likes other boys. Y'know, like to be their boyfriend and to hold their hand and stuff. When I was

> younger I remember wondering how he turned out that way. So I asked him . . ." Students listen intently as Tonia tells her complex story. (Fringe Benefits 2000)

A group of young people are in the middle of a drama workshop on gender roles when the drama leader, Elizabeth O'Hara, formally addresses them:

> "We at Mattel are really excited to have you all here today!" the leader in role begins. "As we all know, Mattel Co. has spent the last several months conducting a nationwide search for the 1998 Brand New Barbie. . . . The search has not been easy, and the demands placed on the woman selected will be great." After a brief explanation, some students are asked to assume the role of young women who might want to be considered as possible role models for the "new" Barbie and to think about the qualities this doll should embody; others are in role as judges; and still others as stockholders. As the judges busily get to work establishing the criteria they will use to "judge" the contestants, and the stockholders consider their investments, the possibility of a meaningful discussion about who shapes gender expectations (and how) begins to percolate. (O'Hara and Lanoux 1998)

In each of these instances, young people are actively encouraged to think about and question various aspects of identity, difference, and the impact of bias. These drama educators and theatre artists have resourced themselves, analyzed the complexities of the identity locations in question, and applied that knowledge to the ways in which they have structured their work. They serve as terrific examples of how drama educators and practitioners can help set the tone for questioning how identity formation works and what happens when different identity positions collide. Our work *can* provide a powerful way to carefully examine how cultural knowledge is constructed—and where bias begins.

Symptoms of Bias

The need for a pluralistic perspective in drama and theatre education is increasingly more apparent as we are reminded daily of the symptoms of bias, ranging from harassment in the form of name-calling and bullying to more insidious hate crimes involving violent attacks and even murder. As Sleeter and Grant (1994) observe, when these symptoms are enacted in classroom situations teachers often "treat the symptoms only—the name-calling, stereotyping, and prejudice" (115). Educators in every arena need to move beyond simply attending to the symptoms and begin to build greater understanding about why these various biased attitudes exist, how bias affects people, the benefits and costs of bias, and what we can do to alleviate it.

During the time I have been thinking about these issues and writing this book, there have been several shocking incidents where open-mindedness was abandoned in favor of brutality: James Byrd, a Black man, was dragged to death behind a truck in Texas; Matthew Shepard, a young gay man, was tied to a fence and beaten to death in Wyoming; young people were targeted and brutally murdered by their peers because of their differences at a school in Littleton, Colorado; and Jewish children were shot at in a day-care center in Los Angeles. The list, sadly, goes on. Of course, there are smaller acts of intolerance every day: no welfare without work, lack of proper access to buildings and cultural events for wheelchair users, conflicts over where day labor camps should (or should *not*) be located, and schools with vastly unequal funding bases.

Each of these acts of blatant and not-so-blatant intolerance is a teaching opportunity. As young people watch the news, hear adults discuss current events, and see pictures in the papers, their attitudes about difference and tolerance are being shaped. I believe it is crucial for those of us working with young people to seize any opportunity we can to overtly discuss and analyze the social mechanisms of bias.

Beyond Tolerance

Increasing tolerance is often the main goal of multicultural education efforts. The problem with the simple goal of "tolerance" is that it often means to endure or to put up with something or someone you do not like or agree with. In my own work, I tend to refigure the notion of tolerance to include some of its other shades of meaning—such as open-mindedness, along with a cluster of associated terms like *allowance, magnanimity, lenity, compassion, progressivism, and generosity,* mixed with analysis and critique. In this book, I am advocating for a pluralistic perspective that is less about what should be tolerated and more about what can *no longer* be tolerated.

The Roadmap

As this book unfolds, I invite you to think with me: How do individual identity locations and social group memberships affect our ideology and pedagogy and ultimately shape our work? How can reflexivity—the critical [re]examination of our experience and beliefs—be a helpful and essential part of responsible educational theatre practice? How can theory and practice work together productively as a way to examine these issues?

The book is organized following Geneva Gay's suggestion that knowledge, attitudes, and skills are needed to help teachers to make significant changes in their practice so they can be as responsive as possible to culturally diverse students (1977). Chapter 1 offers an overview of the complexities of identity formation and social group membership. Each of the subsequent chapters is framed by the "ABC's" of the specific identity location in question: **A**nalyzing the particular area of difference for increased knowledge, **B**uilding awareness with young people as a way to examine attitudes, and **C**reating an environment for equity through tangible pedagogical techniques and skills. Chapter 2 considers race and ethnicity; Chapter 3 examines social class; Chapter 4 looks at the complexities of gender construction; Chapter 5 explores issues related to sexual orientation, and Chapter 6 rethinks the notion of ability. By first considering the constructedness of each of these identity categories we can proceed to rethinking received attitudes and taking action in and through our work.

While this book assumes a reader who has some previous drama experience or knowledge of theatre work with young people, the appendix gives a brief overview and explanation of terminology and approaches. Although not a handbook on how to teach drama *or* how to teach the "culturally different," I hope the questions raised will help us all strengthen and improve our efforts on both fronts in the future. As I attempt to do in my teaching, I have tried to treat this book as an "environment" in and through which readers can ultimately create their own understandings of the pluralistic nature of human encounters and apply these understandings and critical insights to their own practice. I have included questions to ponder, practical problems to consider, and case study situations at the end of each chapter as a way for readers to engage more fully with the material under consideration. I welcome dialogue beyond these pages. E-mail me (sgrady@utxvms.cc.utexas.edu) and each other with your insights, discoveries, and suggestions. Keep adding to this beginning compilation of resources. This book is not intended to be a destination point but a rest stop—a place to reflect and renew along the hard journey toward critical discoveries.

Naming Ourselves and Others

On this journey, how we name ourselves and others matters. I have chosen to use the term *White* for those of us from European backgrounds or descent to help foreground the issue of Whiteness within this exploration. Following Beverly Daniel Tatum (1999), I use the term *people of color* to refer to groups of Americans that have been targets of racism, and *Black* for Americans of African, Afro-Caribbean, or Dominican descent. Following Félix Masud-Piloto (1995), I use *Latina/o* for Americans of Hispanic descent—though this construction is somewhat awkward, I want to be gender inclusive. I use *Amer-*

ican Indian for Native American populations, *Asian Indian* for people from India, and *Asian American* for Americans from Japan, China, and the Pacific Rim. In quotations and references, however, I will retain the terminology used by the original author to indicate race or ethnicity. I recognize that the naming of self and others contains a universe of power dynamics and is doomed to imperfection. My carefulness, however, is part of my desire to confront hard issues as honestly and openly as I can.

"Diversity Is Not a Choice . . ."

An idealized, albeit problematic, desire for democracy is at the heart of any argument for multicultural education—and cannot be ignored as I advocate for a pluralistic perspective. Yes, in the best of all possible worlds, all our students should be able to participate in a kind of "democracy-in-action" throughout their experience of school. But how is the present desire for an "education in democracy" any different from the problematic attempts to assimilate immigrant children at the turn of the century by social reformers? Several harsh critiques have been leveled at those attempts to use the arts to help indoctrinate students into the "American Way of Life" at the expense, of course, of their cultural differences.[1] Simiarly, how do we negotiate between a White middle-class understanding of "success" and differing cultural values? While a grand idea, democracy is fraught with the humanistic desire for wholeness and equality that can never quite be attained because unequal power dynamics are impossible to escape. Perhaps the best we can do is be willing and able to recognize power, acknowledge bias, work toward understanding, and know that it is a constant and daily struggle. By developing our "response-[abilities]" as educational theorist Cynthia Dillard (1996) advocates, we can become "critical shapers" of schools and the society in which we live.

Gary Howard (1999), an educator who has been struggling with multicultural education issues for the past twenty-five years, passionately believes that dealing with diversity is not a choice—but, in his words, "our responses to it certainly are" (2). I hope this book will open up discussion about how we might respond through our practice and pedagogy—regardless of how imperfect and provisional our efforts may be.

Notes

1. For an provocative critique of Alice Minnie Herts and Lillian Wald's educational drama work with immigrants at the turn of the century, see Stephanie Etheridge Woodson (1998) and Patrick Tuite (1998).

Acknowledgments

Any endeavor such as this has the minds, ideas, and arguments of many people echoing through it. The themes I've woven together in this book reflect how a multitude of challenging encounters have resonated through my theorizing and informed my practice. There are oceans of people to thank in this effort: numerous colleagues who attended the American Alliance for Theatre and Education (AATE) conferences in Denver (1998) and Chicago (1999), the Theatre and Social Change focus group sessions at the Association for Theatre in Higher Education conference in Toronto (1999), and the Drama and Theatre in Education Research conference (1999) in Exeter, U.K. for challenging and encouraging me with their feedback on various parts of the manuscript I presented in numerous sessions; colleagues on the AATE College/University Network Listserv who have shared countless resources and stories with me; the scores of elementary students I have worked with and learned from in Kerala, South India, Madison, WI, and Austin, TX; elementary school teachers who have given me much to consider, including Kunju Vasudevan Namboordiripad in Kerala and Janice Lowery and Larry Kirk in Austin. My supportive colleagues at the University of Texas (UT), especially Coleman Jennings, Joan Lazarus, and Suzan Zeder, have patiently helped me carve out the time needed to complete this manuscript. Jill Dolan, my friend and new colleague at UT, generously offered to read initial drafts of the manuscript, as did my dear *amigo* Lorenzo Garcia at the University of North Texas. This work would not have been possible without the financial support provided by funds from the UT College of Fine Arts, University Research Institute, and the Department of Theatre and Dance. In addition, the Central School of Speech and Drama in London and my colleagues Sally Mackey and Pam Shaw provided me with a forum through which to float some of my early writing and thinking—particularly concerning the curious silence surrounding social class in U.S. culture.

Many people graciously allowed me to "pick their brains" about how they think and teach about difference, including British colleagues Andy Kemp, Joe Winston, and Jonothan Neelands, who generously shared their thoughts and opinions. I am extremely grateful to those who shared their specific expertise, including Rachel Briley, Angela Vogler, and Gene Mirus for their insights on ability and ableism. Susan Pearson-Davis generously shared her thoughts about how her early research on cultural diversity has affected her present work. Norma Bowles from Fringe Benefits Theatre Company in Los Angeles shared an exciting draft of her play *Cootie Shots,* as well as her commitment to representing a range of differences in theatre for young people. My friend Judy Matetzschk enthusiastically pointed me to other children's dramatic literature dealing with difference. Gayle Sergel from Dramatic Publishing Company introduced me to several new plays addressing diversity issues. Johnny Saldaña at Arizona State University has been steadfast in his encouragement and has generously shared his lesson plans and units on "Improvisation with the -Isms" as a way to teach for diversity and social justice in the classroom. Elizabeth O'Hara and Carol Lanoux have also shared their lesson plans on gender and the background research informing their work. Undergraduate and graduate students in my classes at UT have asked me challenging questions about these issues along the way and I have benefited enormously from their thoughts and experience. I am especially grateful to Diane Nutting and Amber Feldman for their thoughtful reflections. I am also deeply indebted to Tori January for her tireless efforts as my research assistant; Christine Wong for the cool and calm way she talked me through my multiple computer problems; and my editor, Lisa Barnett, for demystifying the process of publication with good humor and enormous patience.

In addition, my dear friend Helen Nicholson has been a constant source of support and wisdom throughout this process. Her wry wit and needling encouragement helped keep me going. Finally, I'd like to thank my partner and intellectual collaborator, Richard Isackes, who has been the world's best cheerleader—and critic! I'm also extremely grateful to Morgan and Betsy—Richard's daughters and my friends—for talking to me about their experience of the world in sometimes funny and sometimes painful but always perceptive ways. Thank you, all. I have benefited enormously from this collective wisdom. I hope others will, too.

1

Introduction

geographies of difference

"To worry or to smile, such is the choice when we are assailed by the strange; our decision depends on how familiar we are with our own ghosts."

—JULIA KRISTEVA, *STRANGERS TO OURSELVES*

It is my first improvisational drama session with a fourth-grade class of Black and Mexican American students who are passionately trying to convince me, in role as their caregiver, to let them keep a boa constrictor they "found" under rather suspicious circumstances. They try several different approaches, including begging, pouting, reasoning, and promising. I react with a high degree of skepticism and continue to ask why I should allow this creature in my house. Suddenly nine-year-old Miguel jumps up and points an imaginary gun directly at me. "*Now* let's see if you don't let us keep it!" he taunts. All eyes are on Miguel, who is proudly empowered by his imagined weapon. There is an awkward silence.

"Let's stop the drama," I say with my heart pounding. My mind is racing. Where did Miguel learn that guns are a viable way to resolve arguments, even in confrontations with adults? What did I hear about gang activity in this neighborhood? Didn't someone tell me that these children lack parental involvement in their lives? Hold on a second. As a White woman, am I stereotyping here?

"Let's relax for a moment and think about what just happened," I begin, while mentally scrambling for a way to turn this moment into a learning opportunity. "I wonder how you convince someone with more power than you to listen. How do you persuade someone to see things from your perspective?" After a few fits and starts, a lively discussion develops as students eagerly begin sharing stories of previous confrontations with "power."

In this brief "dramatic" exchange, a moment of "difference" between a teacher and her students has been catalogued—along with the myriad of questions and concerns it poses. As my first experience teaching in a low-income Black and Latina/o neighborhood, this improvisational scene raised many questions for me as a drama practitioner. Can creative drama be a valuable teaching tool and art form in *all* elementary classrooms—despite the student population? What guidelines are there for working with and across difference in educational settings? Specifically, what are the most productive ways for teachers using drama as an educational tool to account for and respond to individual and cultural differences in their work with diverse groups of young people?

The difficult journey toward a more reasoned understanding of the differences in question can only begin if assumptions, stereotypes, and rumors are carefully examined. For example, the drama lesson described above was the first of several exploratory improvisational sessions I conducted with this fourth-grade class during the spring of 1996. It was initially designed to extend their language arts curriculum for which they were reading a short story called "Dear Bronx Zoo." My intention was to create a compelling dramatic situation that would blend language arts skills with information about habitat requirements from their science curriculum.

While attention to the curriculum was at the base of this first lesson, our differences proved to be a constant silent presence. The first and most obvious difference had to do with our ethnic backgrounds and cultural identities. As a well-traveled middle-aged White woman who fancied myself as experienced in negotiating difference, I was surprised at the difficulty I had in gaining trust and engaging this group of Black and Latina/o children to "play" along with me. Granted, none of the children had participated in structured drama activities quite like this before, but we were having difficulty finding common ground. A second area of difference had struck me earlier in the day as I drove into the neighborhood and was confronted by the reality of deteriorating subsidized housing projects and street after street of miscellaneous run-down single-family dwellings. There was a palpable disjuncture between the socioeconomic circumstances that affected these students on a daily basis and my own comfortable upper-middle-class rural existence. To further complicate the situation, the White middle-class assumptions that, by and large, inform how school operates and how young people should treat adults was at variance with the prevailing distrust many of these students felt toward White power figures (especially new ones like me). Those in power often translate this distrust as disrespect—an offense for which students of color are routinely punished. (For example, my cooperating classroom teacher—a White male—wanted to send Miguel to the principal for his "in role" defiance! It took me a few minutes to convince him not to. The combination of the "looseness" of drama and our discussions about power made him quite uncomfortable—although he never admitted it.) While approaching the experience of school from very different racial and socioeconomic positions, all of us were just trying to get through the day—and vaguely wondering why it was so difficult.

In our increasingly diverse world, those of us who work with young people either in classroom situations or in performative settings find ourselves constantly negotiating between various territories of difference. Confronting and coexisting with difference is a factor in any social interaction. Assumptions about what is "normal" tend to gloss over these differences and have an enormous impact on what we enable young people to learn and how mindful we are of their diversity. I am defining diversity as a broad range of individual identity markers, including race and ethnicity, gender, social class, and ability. Teachers and practitioners should *not* assume, therefore, that a low number of students of color in their classrooms or audiences excuses them from attending to difference. How many times have limiting assumptions been "naturalized" in drama and theatre work that habitually features male protagonists, female sidekicks, nuclear families, or primitive "natives" in an able-bodied universe? These assumptions erase difference in favor of a dominant culture view of "how things are" or a presumption of how things *should* be—which, at best, are expressed as stereotype or, at worst, as oppression.

As a drama practitioner and educator I have long been interested in the intersections and collisions between drama work and its cultural contexts. This was most clearly evident when I lived in India on several different occasions and subsequently did my master's thesis on the use of creative drama as an educational tool in South Indian schools (Grady 1990). My more recent practical work in Texas in economically disadvantaged neighborhoods and often with students of color has alerted me to the complex workings of differing cultural contexts and the ways in which these differences affect our work. While scholars and practitioners have begun to address multiculturalism in educational drama and theatre practice (Saldaña 1991, Pearson-Davis 1993, Gonzalez 1995, Garcia 1997), attend to gender awareness (Nicholson 1995, Fletcher 1995), and reflect on particular cultural identity issues (Byram and Fleming 1998, Garcia 1998, Wagner 1998), there has been little discussion concerning how drama teachers and theatre practitioners might actively respond to the vast diversity present in our student populations. In this book, I examine the overall implications of diversity and "difference" as a factor in social relations, consider how a better understanding of specific differences might prove useful for working with young people, provide several sample drama lessons as a way to address the complexities of various differences with young people, and argue the need for a pluralistic pedagogical perspective as way to actively acknowledge difference in educational drama and theatre work.

What Is Drama?

Throughout the book I will be citing many examples of process-oriented drama work conducted with elementary school students. Known as "creative drama" by American practitioners or "drama in education" by British colleagues, the kind of drama work described in my opening story relies on the combination of kinesthetic, emotional, and intellectual involvements in improvisational activities to promote a range of experiences from artistic self-expression to active learning in particular curriculum areas.

A "process" approach implies that the work is primarily done for the benefit of the participants, rather than for an audience, in order to more fully examine subject matter, strengthen drama skills, and enhance critical thinking. Drama work embraces many techniques, including games to enhance cooperative strategies, traditional games, and theatre games; story dramatization, in which a piece of literature is enacted improvisationally; process drama, in which a group—including the teacher—collectively embarks on a dramatic adventure by taking on various roles; and Augusto Boal's Theatre of the Oppressed techniques, including image theatre, which focuses on creating still images of concepts or ideas with bodies, as well as forum theatre work, in which improvisational scenes are replayed with various students replacing the protagonist as a way to explore other solutions to the problem under investigation.

Although my main focus will be on dealing with difference in improvisational drama work, I will also refer to the impact of diversity issues on children's theatre, that is, theatre work specifically designed by adults for audiences of young people and their families. As a drama and theatre practitioner, I believe these art forms can move students toward active critical learning in unique ways. Over the years I have become particularly committed to exploring how these improvisational techniques can enhance a variety of subject areas at the elementary school level. Throughout the book, there are several references to drama work that addresses many different curricular topics, including health, science, language arts, social studies, and math. In many instances, these lessons have several cross-curricular components, as was the intention of the drama about the boa constrictor referred to at the beginning of the chapter.

Teaching, however, is not just about pedagogy and method. To be truly effective, teaching involves a heightened awareness of the context in which one is teaching or working. In the broadest sense, context can refer to a nation, region, city, or general neighborhood. In its most particular sense, context can refer to a specific school, classroom, or individual students. "Context-sensitive" teachers or practitioners delicately balance self-awareness, context, pedagogy, and method as they strive toward their educational outcomes. The result is the artistry of teaching.

Difference as a "Foreign" Concept

"Foreignness does not start at the water's edge, but at the skin's."

—*Clifford Geertz, "The Uses of Diversity,"*
from Tanner Lectures on Social Values.

In any human interaction, "difference" is a factor. Our own self-definition grows and changes as we interact with or measure self against "others." We actively differentiate and order the world accordingly, often separating out the foreign from the familiar. The initial scale of measuring difference is often a visual one. According to theorist Paul Gilroy, this scale is generally based on "comparative anatomy" (1997, 193). However, difference occurs at many levels and often cannot be so neatly or easily calibrated. Confronting difference is not always comfortable. One response is to ignore the difference and pretend it doesn't matter; another response is to enter into more self-consciously complex relationships with what we perceive as different or foreign.

In my own practice and theorizing, actively grappling with the "foreign" has helped me understanding the importance of addressing difference. In 1989, for example, I had the opportunity to conduct a workshop with a group of young people from *Rangaprabhath* (literally, "rising sun"), a children's theatre in Kerala, South India. The lively group of forty children, ages five through fourteen, were all from economically poor families of farm laborers.

At that time, my knowledge of Malayalam, the language spoken in Kerala, was insufficient for conducting such an in-depth workshop, so I needed the help of a translator. Together we began with a series of games adapted to suit the context—Red Light/Green Light became "Stop and Go" because stoplights were not widely used in South India at that time. The structure of this activity then grew into various context-sensitive dramatic situations as we in turn became agents from the Central Bureau of Investigation

Figure 1–1. *Young people in Kerala playing Red Light/Green Light.* Photo by Sharon Grady.

(equivalent to the FBI in the U.S.) sneaking up on a crook's hideaway, and then a group of *kuttychatans* (mischievous ghosts) trying to surprise a small child. Similarly, a Blind Walk exercise involved same-sex pairs due to the cultural practice of arranged marriage, which discourages any contact that might invite love matches between males and females.

After pantomiming and discussing various occupations needed to enable a society to function, we then launched into an extended group improvisation about an impending visit by the new Prime Minister who, as a North Indian, had expressed his desire to better understand the diverse people of India's many states. To that end, we imagined that the Prime Minister was on his way to Kerala and students quickly began planning ways to make their unique South Indian culture understandable to this "foreign" other.

This anecdote, at first glance, is a story about what could be considered an "exotic" sort of difference. On the visible level, as a White European American female drama practitioner, I am markedly different from the 40 Indian children with whom I was working. However, there are multiple layers of difference contained within this reflective account. Besides the more obvious racial differences, there are differences embedded in ethnicity and cultural

Figure 1–2. *Young people in Kerala exploring a Blind Walk exercise.* Photo by Sharon Grady.

norms. In this regard, ethnicity can be defined as "a group that is socially distinct or set apart, by others and/or by itself, primarily on the basis of cultural or national characteristics" (Ashcroft, Griffiths, and Tiffin 1998, 81). The term "culture" can be seen as both a description of the material products of a society as well as a theoretical concept that seeks to illuminate how a particular group engages in the production of meaning (Childers and Hentzi 1995, 66). Cultural norms are behaviors that are acceptable to a particular culture. Arranged marriage is a cultural norm I cannot ignore as a drama leader working in an Indian context and necessitates that I deal with gender in ways I might not in my own culture. Further, my economic background and privilege as an upper-middle-class American is a constant presence in our interactions, though I try to downplay my origins by wearing a common Indian *salwar kameez* (long tunic and pajama pants). These low caste Hindu young people wonder about life in America where I have my own house and land and a job at a university. My language and accent also mark me as a privileged "other."

More often than not, drama teachers and theatre practitioners respond to the issue of "difference" or "foreignness" by making it the *subject* of their work—just as I did in India. While this approach is often useful as a way to overtly discuss related issues such as intolerance and exclusion, I also suggest the importance of acknowledging difference (and by extension, diversity) as a *practice.* How might an embodied understanding of difference develop from a critical awareness of self and context? How might this embodied understanding positively inform how we approach our work and those with whom we work?

An "embodied" concept of difference directly affects how teachers and practitioners account for and foreground their own identity or subject positions in their work. Often understandings of our own social positionings are simply taken as givens as the world around us is conveniently "naturalized" according to our own particular ways of seeing. The assumptions about how things should be organized and who should be in charge are often so familiar that we forget that they are not "universal." This situation is compounded when working in various art forms because of the prevailing sentiment that the arts are "universal." However, what we assume as natural, universal, and commonplace is in actuality "foreign" to many others. To what degree are we all foreigners to someone else in this regard?

How one takes up the challenge of the "foreign" is key to an understanding of how we might deal with difference more effectively in educational drama and theatre. It is not enough to simply and uncritically "Celebrate difference!" By examining our own areas of difference, heightening our awareness to context, engaging in meaningful conversations about difference with others, and analyzing various differences and wondering at what points they shift from variation to oppression, we can take the first steps toward diversity as an embodied practice.

Mapping the Self: Identity and Group Membership

Individual subjectivity (or the coordinates that map our identity locations within the larger geographies of difference) is not completely individual—despite the rhetoric of Western individualism. Instead, individual identity locations have been usefully theorized as constructed by and in relationship to other groups with which we share membership. This is not to say that all members of a social grouping can be reduced to simple generalities. Rather, subjectivity is a dynamic process in which individuals alternately comply with and/or resist their socially constructed identities. For example, it can be ar-

SOCIAL IDENTITIES	EXAMPLES OF SOCIAL GROUP MEMBERSHIP
RACE	Black, White, Asian, Latino/a, Native American, Pacific Islander, Biracial
GENDER	male, female, transgender
CLASS	poor, working class, middle class, owning class
PHYSICAL/MENTAL/ DEVELOPMENTAL ABILITY	able, disabled
SEXUAL ORIENTATION	lesbian, gay, bisexual, heterosexual, asexual
RELIGION	Catholic, Jew, Protestant, Buddhist, Hindu, Muslim
AGE	young people, young adults, middle-aged adults, old people

Figure 1–3. *Examples of Social Group Memberships—from* Teaching for Diversity and Social Justice, *(Griffin 1997, 80).*

gued that what it means to be a woman in American culture has been socially constructed by dominant patriarchal and economic interests. Women, therefore, actively negotiate their subjective identities from within such social group constructions and either choose to comply with or resist these normative constructions.

In *Teaching for Diversity and Social Justice,* Pat Griffin's introductory module on identity offers several examples of how individuals locate themselves as members of various social groupings (see Figure 1-3). Basic categories include race, social class, gender, sexual orientation, ability, age, and religion. As mentioned earlier, a distinction can be made between race and ethnicity. Duane Campbell argues that the racial term *Black,* which can be applied to not only African Americans but also to various immigrant groups such as Haitians, Dominicans, and Puerto Ricans, is different from the term *African American,* which designates a distinct ethnic and cultural group (1996, xxxi).

Ethnic and cultural groups, according to sociologist Peter Rose (1997), frequently share such specific identifiers such as language, religion, patterns of family life, and other unique customs (13). The following Social Group Membership Profile can provide a way to begin the process of mapping your own identity coordinates and orienting yourself within the social landscape:

Personal Social Group Membership Profile

Social Identities	Membership	Status
Race		
Gender		
Class		
Ability/Disability		
Sexual Orientation		
Religion		
Age		

Figure 1–4. *Personal Social Group Membership Profile—adapted from* Teaching for Diversity and Social Justice *(Griffin 1997, 80).*

The status of an individual's membership in a group is measured against what is perceived to be the norm of the prevailing or hegemonic culture. For example, the normative culture in the U.S. is generally assumed to be controlled by rich White male heterosexuals who are middle-aged able-bodied Christians. Anything outside the "norm" is often classified as "disadvantaged," "inferior," "discriminated against," or "needing help" (Griffin 1997, 72). Identity politics come into play when these normative assumptions are seen as oppressive to individuals in non-normative social groupings. The degree of oppression one feels depends on the number (one, several, all) of these non-normative identity locations that an individual possesses.

The impact of this oppression in educational settings has been a focus for many educational theorists.[1] The conflict between teacher and student social identities and assumed cultural norms directly affects what students have the opportunity to learn and therefore the degree to which they succeed or fail in the institution of school. The recent flurry of theorizing and debate about multicultural education has helped provide an analysis of and an antidote to exclusionary teaching practices along with attention to the social reconstruction of the educational process.

What Is Multiculturalism?

James Banks has been one of the strongest advocates of the importance of multicultural education in an increasingly diverse world. Banks (1999) argues that multiculturalism is "a reform movement designed to make some major changes in the education of students." He clarifies:

> Multicultural education assumes that race, ethnicity, culture, and social class are salient parts of U.S. society. . . . This diversity also enriches a society by providing all citizens with more opportunities to experience other cultures and thus to become more fulfilled as human beings. (1)

How educators implement a multicultural agenda is a matter of great debate. In *Making Choices for Multicultural Education,* Christine Sleeter and Carl Grant (1994) outline five different approaches to multicultural education as it is currently practiced in the U.S.: 1) Teaching the Culturally Different, 2) Human Relations, 3) Single Group Studies, 4) Multicultural Education, and 5) Multicultural and Social Reconstructionist.

The first approach focuses on the desire to improve the achievement levels of students of color. This attention to "Teaching the Culturally Different" seeks to identify culturally compatible education methods that will raise the success rates of female, poor, "minority," and special needs students within the existing school system. The main thrust of this approach is to help students who are "different" become as "mainstream" as possible so they have a greater chance of playing a productive role in the existing society (Sleeter and Grant 1994, 44). The prevailing assumption is that there is something deficient in some aspect of the cultural experience of these students that limits their ability to succeed according to the "norm." Attention to learning styles, language proficiency, and remedial education is seen as the solution to help these students "catch up" with their more "advantaged" peers. While heavily endorsed by politicians and superintendents, this approach has been critiqued harshly for its assimilationist goals and is not the strategy most multicultural educators champion at present.

The Human Relations approach targets all children with an eye toward promoting unity, tolerance, and acceptance of difference between students. Much of the curriculum focuses on sensitivity training, with strategically deployed lessons on stereotyping, name-calling, and individual differences (Sleeter and Grant 1994, 86). In particular, the contributions of people of color and women are promoted. This approach, while vital in promoting awareness of difference, tends to leave an understanding of difference at the "I'm OK, You're OK" level or, as Christine Sleeter characterizes, "we are all the same because we are different" (1996, 6). Sleeter also notes that this approach resonates best with political beliefs of most White teachers (6). Interestingly, a prominent method in this approach is role-playing. Sleeter and Grant (1994) remark:

> Vicarious experiences can also reduce social distance and develop feelings for empathy. For example, a boy who plays the role of a woman trying to raise a family single-handedly on a secretary's salary may reevaluate his

> stereotypes about working women as well as discover the problems such women face and feel more concern for their situation. (109–110)

However, they caution that this kind of role work can unfortunately oversimplify a situation or context and lead students to believe that resolving large social problems such as racism and sexism is simple matter of just finding ways of "getting along."

Single Group Studies give all students an in-depth understanding of a particular group's oppression with curricula organized around specific groups such as Black Studies, Chicano Studies, Women's Studies, Gay and Lesbian Studies. Students examine how oppression has historically occurred and how members of the group in question currently experience it. The strength of this approach is the re-theorizing of various disciplines from standpoints other than those of European American men (Sleeter 1996, 6). It also clearly argues that the educational process is not neutral (Sleeter and Grant 1994, 129). Rather, all social practices, including the institution of school, are seen to be organized in ways that favor the normative group and discriminate against "others."

According to Sleeter and Grant, work self-consciously identified as Multicultural Education seeks to "promote social structural equality and cultural pluralism" (1994, 171). School is envisioned as a place to rehearse basic democratic principles with the intent of reforming school structures so that democracy and pluralism can more effectively be practiced. Advocates of this approach have been very active in curriculum reform, promoting parent involvement in schools and providing strong critiques of accepted school practices such as tracking.[2]

Finally, the Multicultural and Social Reconstructionist approach to education builds on the former with the important addition of teaching young people to how to take social action for themselves. Not only does school help all students understand how a democracy should work, it teaches them to analyze various forms of political and economic oppression as well as discrimination around them with a focus on how to take action against such oppressive forces (Sleeter and Grant 1994, 211).

These various approaches differ primarily in the degree to which they theorize social practices and advocate for social action. Because of the huge differences in these approaches, there has been a great deal of debate over which approach, or combination of approaches, is most useful. There is also a need, as Christine Sleeter (1996) points out, to distinguish between these various approaches and superficial understandings and practices of multiculturalism (7). For example, Single Group Studies has often been accused of presenting a "touristic" treatment of the social group in question if the focus is only on food, music, stories, unusual customs, or dances. Any attention to the complexities of cultural experience or the political struggles of a group is often eliminated. This, unfortunately, is how many educational drama and theatre practitioners tend to approach cultural difference.

The field of educational drama and theatre is just beginning to explore how multicultural education might apply to various aspects of our work. Johnny Saldaña offers an excellent application of multicultural principles in practical drama work in his book *Drama of Color: Improvisation with Multiethnic Folklore* (1995). Anita Manley and Cecily O'Neill's *Dreamseekers: Creative Approaches to the African American Heritage* (1997) provides substantive historical, artistic, and literary source material and lesson ideas for educational work on African American culture. Nancy Swortzell and Mark Riherd's 1996 essay, "Multiculturalism and Educational Theatre," sheds light on how both drama and interactive theatre-in-education can approach the subject of diversity in various ways. Lorenzo Garcia (1997) has focused on how a multicultural and social reconstructionist approach might usefully inform preservice teachers of theatre arts.

As a theoretical framework to help inform practice, multicultural and social reconstructionist education theory can be viewed as an important way to resist and challenge oppressive social relationships. These theories provide a mechanism for examining diversity and bias in a variety of forms, including White privilege, patriarchal proscriptions, and ableist presumptions. Multicultural education in practice helps acknowledge difference openly and renders it less foreign by respectfully confronting the "strange." This theoretical framework has much to offer educational drama and theatre practitioners desiring to actively "embody" the practice of pluralism.

Multiculturalism, however, is not without detractors. Multicultural education is suspect to some because of its baseline belief in an idealized utopian view of democracy in which no citizen oppresses another. Various contemporary literary theories, such as those associated with postmodernism, have posited that power is pervasive in any human interaction, truth is situated and not absolute or universal, and that identities are extremely unstable and always in flux. With these "givens," the utopian desire for equality is highly questionable if not impossible to achieve. Postmodern theorizing of this kind has itself been strongly criticized for its lack of possibility for or agenda regarding social change. While offering a strong critique of power and oppression, postmodern thinking is accused of proposing nothing beyond analysis. Peter McLaren (1994) has attempted to make a distinction between what he calls "ludic" or neoconservative postmodernism, which makes substantive social critique but "often reinscribes the status quo" (198), and what he calls "resistance" postmodernism. Resistance postmodernism makes use of both the postmodern critiques of power, authority, and truth and the activist agendas of social change. This signals a useful blending of *theory* and *action.*

However, within the desire to "help" those most oppressed by our current sociopolitical climate, there is still the troubling question of how to avoid reinforcing oppressive relationships. Postcolonial critic Gayatri Spivak (1990) has questioned "a certain sort of benevolence towards others" by those who presume that their understanding of the world will "liberate" those they deem less fortunate (19). How do we make sure our own "ethic of help" is not merely another "colonizing" stance that disregards the wishes, desires, and needs of young people and the communities of difference they represent in favor of our own agendas and desires to either "protect," "empower," or "normalize" them?

A Closer Look at Our Field

My concern with the importance of examining and theorizing difference in our practice must be understood within the larger scope of the field of drama and theatre for young people. The "feel-good" factor is still alive and well in much drama and theatre for youth in the U.S., with productions (more often than not) about fantasy creatures and animals derived from European American fairy and folk tales. Barney is a logical outcome. While not overtly "evil," these theatre events have little if any connection to the lives of many of the young people watching them. This kind of theatre is more often about the producers and their dominant culture motivations than the audiences it is supposedly serving. Moses Goldberg has written that those who tend to work in children's theatre should have the desire to "bring" something to children, and do so out of a kind of humanist idealism:

> Perhaps because it is a way of influencing the development of mankind; and is, therefore, a kind of immortality. Perhaps it is an attempt to salvage values, ethics, or morality from the kaleidoscope of modern technological confusion. Perhaps it is a sincere desire to help children to become their unique selves. (1974, 1)

Unfortunately, this idealism is shaped by dominant culture assumptions and usually translates into polarized enactments of good and evil, in which good triumphs and then we all go home. Only a handful of playwrights for young audiences have begun dealing with the grey areas in this very black-and-white vision of the world.

A major theme in much of the discourse about children's theatre has to do with the "act" of corralling children as spectators. Some believe that the mere fact that children have been to the theatre and that their "aesthetic education" is beginning is a good thing. They will most certainly then attend theatre when they are adults—won't they? In *A Good Night Out,* John McGrath (1981, 2) makes it clear that professional theatre is most often performed for a very small elite who are accustomed to seeing *their* stories reflected and not those of the general public. When a child's initial theatre experiences bear little or no resemblance to his or her life experiences, what about it would inspire future visits?

With the publication of the National Standards for Arts Education (which include dance, music, theatre, and visual arts), many in the field have begun earnestly advocating for "what our children must *know* and be able to *do*" in the arts (Consortium of National Arts Education Associations 1994, 60). While offered only for voluntary adoption at this time, these standards present the dominant culture's view of "art" and are pursued with an evangelical zeal in states such as Texas, where there is already a mandate for theatre arts to be taught from kindergarten through grade twelve. However, since it is rare to have theatre arts specialists in elementary schools, documenting and confirming that the prescribed theatre arts curriculum is really being taught can be a vexing problem. Lists, guidelines, and reminders about theatre bombard Texas teachers—but such information rarely points out that the tools of theatre can be quite useful for teaching other subjects. In fact, when questioned at an organizational meeting, the then-theatre coordinator for the Texas Education Agency told me that she worries about "regular" teachers using theatre to teach other subjects because it just isn't "theatre" anymore when they do that. "And besides," she posited, "they do it so badly!"

While laudable for its attention to access and entitlement to the arts, what "every student should know" about theatre strikes me as just as problematic as the culturally biased assumptions of E. D. Hirsh's *Cultural Literacy: What Every American Needs to Know* (1987). Theatre evangelists seldom ask *why* students should know these things or what the nature of "learning" entails. Yet they are quick to counter my concerns by reminding me, as someone did recently, that there is great value in using four different versions of *Hamlet* as a way to show students that there are several ways to solve a problem, in this case the problem of how to produce a "great" piece of literature. Dominant cultural values about "great art" often completely erase the experience of culturally diverse young people.

Process-oriented creative drama has most often been connected to the above aesthetic crusades in the U.S. by exposing students to the basic tenets of theatre. Lessons which often consist of a series of skill-based activities (sensory awareness, creative movement, improvisation) strung together and reflected on in terms of the effectiveness of performance skills. However, British practitioners Dorothy Heathcote, Gavin Bolton, Cecily O'Neill, and others have called attention to the potential for learning associated with this art form by working both *in* and *through* drama in what has become known as "process drama" work. For example, instead of basing the above problem-solving example on *Hamlet,* one possible variation might be an improvisational drama in which students actively create crucial moments of a tense situation of their choosing. These moments are played and discussed as a way to carefully examine choices and consequences. Their "stake" in the ownership of this work allows students to actively examine the roles of identity and context while solving problems that matter to them. At the same time, they strengthen their drama skills (such as character- and scenario-building) and social skills (such as persuasion and debate.)

Concurrent learning happens accidentally all the time, and as drama teachers and practitioners, we have the opportunity to actively structure educational situations in which synchronous learning can purposefully occur. Instead of insisting on bounded disciplinarity, we can engage in process-oriented work that honors the issues that are important to our diverse learners and allows for and encourages frank discussion of our various individual and social identities. This openness, in turn, helps us as a nation successfully meet the challenge of diversity and pluralism in the twenty-first century.

Of course, this project is fraught with complexity. Questions lurk: How can I initiate discussion about such personal issues in the classroom or theatre studio? How will I make sure students stay on task and approach the work seriously? How do I avoid becoming oppressive because of my desire to help? In a critique of her own struggles to create "empowering" classroom environments, Elizabeth Ellsworth (1989) offers this insight:

> If you can talk in ways that show you understand that your knowledge of me, the world, and the right thing to do will always be partial, interested, and potentially oppressive to others, and if I can do the same, then we can work together on shaping and reshaping alliances for constructing circumstances in which students of difference can thrive. (324)

Instead of presuming the correctness of our positions, the grace and humility of reflexivity can serve as an antidote to colonizing behavior and discourse. How do we summon the courage to begin? We start by starting.

Developing a Pluralistic Perspective

Why is a pluralistic perspective needed in the field of drama and theatre for young people? We all have horror stories of practice. I have sometimes noticed a certain apprehension in my White middle-class college students when they are asked to conduct school observations in economically disadvantaged neighborhoods. Their preconceptions about African American and Latina/o students and what "that" neighborhood is like causes them to worry whether they'll come back unscathed. I've witnessed far too many drama lessons that had no connection with (or recognition of) culturally diverse groups of students—where White middle-class views of the world were assumed to be the "universal" experience for contexts in which they simply were not. I've watched and participated in countless dramas that relegate girls and women to stereotypical gender roles. I've seen White teachers completely misread the cultural codes of their students of color and blame the students instead of their own ignorance. I've witnessed what Joyce King (1991) calls "dysconscious racism" as teachers or practitioners tell me they "just don't see color." I've felt the sting of discomfort as I faced young people with various disabilities and attempted to carry on as if nothing needed to be adjusted.

By embodying the practice of diversity—which involves self-consciously interrogating our own identity locations (including race, social class, gender, ability, and sexual orientation) and heightening our context sensitivity as we attend to the complex identities of our students and our audiences—I believe we will be able to more confidently respond to diversity in the young people we find ourselves working with. Further, as we continue to create learning opportunities through drama work, our new understandings will usefully inform discussions of how diversity is represented or erased in a variety of venues. This kind of literacy is invaluable in our increasingly diverse world.

But Isn't This Just a Politically Correct Harangue?

While some might posit that this argument is based on a simple desire to indoctrinate teachers and practitioners into a so-called politically correct stance, I would counter that the accusation of "political correctness" is yet another tactic that those in dominant power positions use to avoid yielding ground. The most verbally vitriolic are generally those who are threatened or at least sense that they have something to lose.

All things considered, finding ways of attending to cultural difference is not a new phenomenon. Culture has always been thickly diverse, yet this fact is often unacknowledged because various configurations of power have downplayed the importance of acknowledging diversity as a positive attribute. The current resistance to redressing this situation is not completely surprising. Lynne Diaz-Rico (1998) explains that when political liberals in the 1980s began using "noninflammatory" labels for minority groups, the terms "became synonymous with the externalizing of positive intent toward issues such as equal opportunity for minorities" (73). At the time of her writing, she notes, the term "political correctness" is used in a highly derogatory manner, as if eliminating pejorative references and inflammatory speech is no longer a worthy pursuit (78). Those labeled "P.C." are seen as caricatures of leftist intellectuals who overreact and "can't take a joke." At what point, however, are we as educators and theatre workers willing to publicly take a stand against cultural misinformation and bigotry?

As drama practitioners become increasingly aware of the complex workings of difference, more self-consciously inclusive teaching and performance strategies are needed. Following Gloria Ladson-Billings' (1994) call for "culturally relevant" teaching practices, strategies for acting on emergent understandings of difference in drama practice and pedagogical perspectives need to be discussed. I argue that instead of just approaching "difference" as an occasional topic in drama and theatre work for young people, attention to difference should be viewed as central to how drama practitioners conceive of their work and conduct their practice.

Telling Stories: Reflective Practice Through Ethnographic Moments

One method I use to map my own orientations to "difference" as a lived practice is to create ethnographic accounts, what anthropologist Clifford Geertz (1973) calls the "thick description" of an event in time and the cultures that perceived it. The term "ethnography" has been used by anthropologists, social scientists, and more recently by educational researchers to describe studies that use techniques such as participant observation, naturalistic inquiry, and open-ended research. These methods result in the narrative description of the culture of a community or society. I follow Gilmore and Smith in their assertion that what ethnography might bring to education and, in turn, educational theatre is not answers, but a "listening, learning posture" that can expand our understanding of our work and the vast geographies of difference that we and our student participants and audiences bring to it (1982, 5).

In various places in this book, I attempt to capture moments of drama practice, which are then analyzed through a constellation of theoretical perspectives on difference (including multicultural, postcolonial, feminist, and disability theory). These theorized stories graphically illustrate the silences and misunderstandings that result from vastly different cultural assumptions between teachers and their students as well as between performers and their audiences. Like the holographic metaphor Lincoln and Guba (1985) evoke in *Naturalistic Inquiry*, I want these stories to hover in the way a three-dimensional holographic image hovers between the interference patterns of two laser beams (56). Like the "interaction and differentiation" that causes holographic images to be made visible, my hope is that these stories will invite recognition and puzzlement as the fragments suggest larger implications—just as the parts of laser images contain a conception of the whole. I am not interested in simple two-dimensional retellings of what happened when, but rather in multilayered accounts with depth and perspectives that shift our easily understood notions of academic space as distant and other.

Ruth Behar (1996) notes that the success of ethnographic work depends on the nature of the relationships formed by a particular researcher with a particular set of people in a particular context. It is vexed, she says, "with the question of vulnerability" (5). She notes Clifford Geertz's suggestion that ethnographies are an interesting cross between "author-saturated and author-evacuated texts, neither romance nor lab report, but something in between" (7). This book is intensely author saturated—an exercise in vulnerability. But not to worry—I have followed Behar's advice carefully. What is included here is an exposure of self only insofar as it takes us collectively "somewhere we couldn't get to otherwise" (14). It is essential to my argument and not "decorative flourish" or "exposure for its own sake" (14). Behar goes on to state that this kind of personal investment makes the work worth doing:

> Call it sentimental, call it Victorian and nineteenth century, but I say that anthropology that doesn't break your heart just isn't worth doing anymore. (177)

And, with apologies to Behar, I believe that educational drama practice that doesn't "break your heart"—that doesn't passionately involve your heart and intellect—just isn't worth doing, either.

Against this matrix, I propose the difficult task of locating ourselves within the larger social landscape and the geographies of difference. How are our various locations related and overlapping? At what points are they vastly different? What do your orientations reveal about your status? As individual and social beings we are always on the move. What is it that causes our identity coordinates to shift and change? Although the metaphor of mapping may not be sufficient to contain the complexities of identity, cartographer Denis Wood (1992) contends that maps can represent "the milieu we simultaneously live in and collaborate on bringing [into] being" (1). They embody, he continues, an interested selectivity of "presences and absences." In this regard, how can maps help us metaphorically describe the "presences and absences" of identity?

Questions to Ponder

1. How would you identify the social groupings of which you are a member?
2. How would you characterize your status vis-à-vis other members of your particular social groupings?

3. How would you characterize your status vis-à-vis the young people you ordinarily work with?
4. What disjunctures can you imagine might occur between your identity locations and your students' identity locations?
5. What situations can you imagine in which identity location and social group membership affect your students or your student audiences either negatively or positively?

Practical Problems to Consider

1. A mobility-impaired student who uses a wheelchair has just joined your afterschool drama class. The other students are curious but uncomfortable and tend to avoid her. How might you structure an activity that could help everyone feel more at ease?
2. Your principal or company director wants you to organize a multicultural event and suggests featuring dances, food, and traditional costumes from several different countries. How do you plan a program that includes a more complex understanding of difference?
3. Students in your class continually make stereotypical gender role and sexual orientation assumptions about the characters they create in their improvisational work. How might you intervene or open up discussion?
4. Students in your class are relatively homogeneous in terms of race, social class, and ability. When discussing and improvising a situation involving a very different race, class, or ability group they display blatant stereotypical behavior. How do you handle the situation?
5. Your school or theatre group has been discussing "difference" as a theme for its upcoming original production. A tentative title, "We're All Different and It's OK," has been chosen as a place to begin improvisational work. What improvisational activities might you suggest to deepen your discussions about this topic?

A Case Study Situation

You have been asked to assist with the creation of outreach materials for a theatre company's production of *The Miracle Worker*, about Helen Keller and her teacher Anne Sullivan. These materials are to consist of a twelve-page resource guide for teachers as well as a forty-five-minute postshow workshop for fourth-grade students that explores some of the play's issues and themes.

Describe how you might accomplish both tasks while keeping in mind the diversity (race, class, gender, and ability) of your various student audiences.

Notes

1. See, for example, Ellsworth (1989), Apple (1990), and Giroux (1992) among others.

2. *Tracking* is the practice of grouping students according to perceived or tested abilities. These separate classes for gifted or high-performing students and for low-performing students are often divided by race and social class and are believed to further entrench discrimination and unequal access to learning.

2

Racial and Ethnic Orientations

the problem of privilege

"It is not difference itself that leads to subordination, but the interpretation of difference."

—PAULA ROTHENBERG, *RACE, CLASS, GENDER IN THE UNITED STATES.*

Very early in my graduate career at the University of Wisconsin, I was the teacher of record for a creative drama course required of all elementary education majors. At a planning meeting for an upcoming drama lesson that would be taught to our afterschool lab group of second and third graders, two very sincere White college students were interested in doing a Thanksgiving drama—reenacting the supposed first feast and the coming together of the Pilgrims and American Indians. I outlined the problems they would need to take on board, including the tendency of "well-meaning" individuals to stereotype American Indians as simple "ritual making" others. How could they more carefully examine the feelings (and fears) the Pilgrims and the native people might have about each other as well as the power dynamics inherent in the encounter? They said they would certainly take it into consideration.

On their assigned day, the lesson began as the college students greeted the children on the first floor of the building in order to escort them to our basement drama room. The teachers immediately handed out headbands with two paper feathers to all of the children. I sighed and made a note about the predictable stereotyped behavior that followed. On our circuitous journey downstairs, a treasure hunt unfolded with clues about the day's lesson hidden in various places along the way. I took up the rear already wondering how on earth I would critique this lesson in a way that the college students would be able to hear and understand.

As the group of young people and college students turned the corner and were making their way to our room, they unexpectedly encountered a "real" American Indian who just happened to be on the premises for an interview at the public TV studio also located in the basement. The panicked drama leaders ran back to me and whispered, "There's a real Indian in the building! What are we going to do?" "Why does that bother you?" I asked. "Because . . . well, because," one stammered, "he might think that we're making fun of his culture." "You're right," I said quietly, "he just might." Sheepishly, they gathered the children and quickly steered them into the classroom for the rest of the lesson.

However humbling, the experience of having to confront this "authentic" presence while playing his stereotype immediately focused the critique of this session on how drama teachers and theatre practitioners of various racial and ethnic backgrounds (in this case, White) represent and honor cultural experiences different from our own in our work with young people. How can we actively avoid reinforcing negative stereotypes in our work—and thereby interrupt negative constructions of knowledge about "others"?

ABC's of Race and Ethnicity

Analyzing race and ethnicity as identity locations requires a close look at the ways in which these terms have been defined. What are we to make of the fact that various racial identifiers (such as "Black") shift and change depending on particular cultural contexts? In this chapter, I examine the socially constructed notion of race as a political and cultural phenomenon defined in relation to "Whiteness" and "White" privilege. I also consider the degree to which parents, teachers, and forms of popular culture such as theatre and drama pass on understandings of privilege and perpetuate bias. I will carefully weight the impact of racial bias in several arenas, paying particular attention to how bias affects student achievement. As the student population becomes increasingly more diverse, the majority of the teaching force continues to consist of White, middle-class, English-speaking women. According to Gloria Ladson-Billings, less than 5 percent of teachers are African American (1994, x). I argue that it is time for White teachers and theatre practitioners to enter into critical discussions about the complexities of race and racial bias with our culturally diverse students and colleagues so we can move toward the creation of positive racial identities that are not solely based on the dynamics of privilege.

Building an awareness of race and racial bias through classroom drama work is illustrated in two age-appropriate lesson plans using a variety of drama techniques. Younger elementary students openly ponder the many different ways people can be grouped, including by color. Reading the story *The Colors of Us*, students meet Lena, who is puzzling over the various colors of the people she meets. Students in the upper elementary range are challenged to help find a solution when a neighborhood experiences racial tensions in *Smoky Night*.

The final part of the chapter lists several ideas for creating a classroom environment or theatre work that acknowledges the problem of racial privilege and bias and works against its perpetuation. Teachers and theatre makers are encouraged to confront their own relationship to race and carefully monitor the messages we send and assumptions we make.

Analyzing Race

According to my dictionary, race is defined as:

> 1: a breeding stock of animals
> 2a: a family, tribe, people, or nation belonging to the same stock; b: a class or kind of people unified by a community of interests, habits, or characteristics
> 3a: an actually or potentially interbreeding group within a species; b: BREED; c: a division of mankind possessing traits that are transmissible by descent and sufficient to characterize it as a distinct human type. (*Webster's Ninth Collegiate Dictionary* 1990, 969)

Attention to "breed" and "breeding," Michael Banton argues, was one of the first ways humans tried to answer the question "Why are they not like us?" According to Banton, species differences, racial traits and types, and genetic variation have all be used as ways for humans to sort themselves physically and culturally (quoted in Payne 1995, 449).

Multicultural educators Donna Gollnick and Philip Chinn tell us that "race" is a concept developed by anthropologists to help them catalog and characterize the physical differences and characteristics of the peoples of the world (1998, 85). Historically, however, there has been much contention between anthropologists over how many races exist. Brewton Berry's 1942 essay "A Southerner Learns about Race" situates the dilemma:

> Hardly two [scientists] agree as to the number and composition of the races. Thus one scholar makes an elaborate classification of twenty-nine

> races; another tells us there are six; Huxley gives us four; Kroeber three; Goldenweiser, five; and Boas inclines to two, while his colleague, Linton, says there are twelve or fifteen. (Quoted in Jacobson 1998, xi)

Clearly, the absence of agreement begins to raise questions about what "race" really means and who is defining it.

In common usage, *race* has come to mean the observable physical characteristics that denote different racial groups. While multicultural educators Duane Campbell and Manning Marable situate *race* as a term that describes a "large group of people with a somewhat similar genetic history," they are careful to point to the fallacy of this artificial grouping by stressing that there is no such thing as genetic purity (1996, 49). The problem with locating race simply as shared genetic history is that, due to migration and transcultural flow, there has been an extraordinary amount of "mixing" in various human populations, resulting in more variation within racial groups than between them (Wijeyesinghe, et al. 1997, 82). Often what is referred to as "race" has more to do with assumptions or stereotypes about cultural difference or ethnicity than with any essential biological differences (Omi and Winant 1994).

A further complication arises when one compares how race is discussed in different cultural contexts. While the immediate racial categories identified in the 1990 U.S. census (Black, White, Asian, and Hispanic) conjure up a certain set of meanings about racial diversity in an American context, the meaning of these categories shifts in different cultural contexts. In England, for example, "Black" can refer to someone of Indian or Pakistani descent, whereas in an American context "Black" most commonly refers to someone of African descent. Race as a concept, therefore, can be understood to be culturally and socially constructed.

In *Whiteness of a Different Color,* Matthew Frye Jacobson argues that "race" is an invented identity category, a designation "coined for the sake of grouping and separating peoples along lines of presumed difference" (1998, 4). Paraphrasing Simone de Beauvoir's assessment of the social category of "woman," he asserts that "Caucasians are made and not born" as he considers the historic changeability of racial categories in different contexts. In racial matters, he asserts, the eye that sees is "a means of perception conditioned by the tradition in which the possessor has been reared" (10). Our own racial positioning socializes us to think in particular ways about race. This racial socialization permeates our thinking whether we are conscious of it or not.

Race resides, then, not in nature but in politics and culture, as Jacobson insists (9). In the history of the U.S., race was a key factor in determining citizenship because the Constitution overtly stipulated that only "free white" immigrants could be granted that privilege. Under the strain of increasing numbers of immigrants, racial understandings and categories began to shift and change as questions arose over which of the new immigrants were fit for self-government and which were not.[1] Today political debate rages over the degree to which racial categories should be considered in policies concerning affirmative action, immigration, welfare, and access to education and which should not. Should economic circumstances be more of a determinant? Can access to economic success be separated from racial identity? What does this begin to suggest about the relationship between race and privilege?

The Struggle Between Race, Ethnicity, and Privilege. While the socially constructed category of "race" has to do with observable characteristics such as skin color, it is generally distinguished from ethnicity, which includes more specific identity markers such as nationality, national origins or ancestry, and religious affiliation (Robles de Meléndez and Ostertag 1997, 62). These distinctions are also constructed and dependent on context. When asked directly about racial background or racial identity, many White Americans immediately self-identify with a long-ago ethnic past—possibly as a way to distance themselves from the question of race. Jacobson relates an incident about an African American leader of a racism seminar who noticed students explaining away their Whiteness in favor of ethnicity with comments such as "I'm not white, I'm Italian" (7). Finally the seminar leader asked, "Where are all the white people who were here just a minute ago?" Counseling psychologist Janet Helms considers this "White flight" a symptom of the confusion over the difference between race and ethnicity and points out that generally an individual has both—whether or not they are consciously aware of both (11). Helms points out that many Whites describe themselves as "mongrels" or "nothing" which, she asserts, is partially due to acculturation and assimilation. I have noticed this tendency in my own classes as some university students ardently insist they have no cultural roots or moorings. "I'm an American," one young woman recently pleaded in class, "why do I have to feel bad about that?" Why *do* discussions about race bring up such strong negative connotations for many Whites?

Whiteness in the U.S. carries with it a certain kind of privilege that is difficult to ignore. The historical reality of slavery, one of the most extreme forms of racial bias, is still unsettling for most. Jacobson cogently points to the fact that this country was founded on White privilege and White governance. Regardless of the socioeconomic level a White person is born into, he or she automatically has access to that legacy of White privilege. The problem with privilege, however, is that one set of experiences is overly valued and all others are undervalued.

Beliefs, Customs, and Attitudes	Manifestation
The importance of the individual	Self-sufficiency and individual achievement is highly valued.
Individual control over destiny	Homeless people have chosen their fate; the unemployed do not want to work.
The ideal "nuclear" family	Alternate family situations (single parents, etc.) are viewed as abnormal and lacking.
The importance of reason	Emotions are not appropriate in the public arena.
Time as a commodity	Time is to be saved or spent well and certainly not wasted.
The Euro-standard of beauty	Appearance is judged by an idealized European vision of what is beautiful.
Universal values	The classics are good enough for all; multicultural education may detract attention from European-based values.
White history as the yardstick	Token weeks and months for other racial groups.
Competitive spirit	Individuals must compete to get ahead; includes test scores, resources, and jobs

Figure 2–1. *Some Beliefs, Customs, and Attitudes of White Culture.*

Mainstream U.S. culture operates on a series of assumptions based on several aspects of White culture, including some very specific customs, beliefs, and attitudes. Figure 2–1 summarizes what Janet Helms sees as the most salient of these societal dimensions and the ways in which they are expressesd in American culture. Helms believes that White people have been able to thrive because of their adherence to these often unspoken and taken-for-granted rules, attitudes, and beliefs (14). As is obvious from this chart, these socially accepted attitudes have a direct impact on the opportunities for success available to people from other racial categories. Anything perceived as deviating from the norm is not valued or is devalued. This has serious implications not only for nondominant racial positions, but also for other identity categories such as gender, sexual orientation, and ability. While White people have flourished because of a society organized around White privilege, they have done so by upholding a policy that devalues other racial categories. Racial bias has a profound impact on the ways in which American society operates. Whether expressed in overt or covert ways, the phenomenon of racism is directly linked to the unease White people have about discussing their own racial identity.

In his book *Portraits of White Racism,* David Wellman defines racism as a "system of advantage based on race" (quoted in Tatum 1999, 7). This definition, as Beverly Daniel Tatum argues, is useful because it clearly situates racism as a phenomenon that goes beyond personal responses to difference and encompasses "a system involving cultural messages and institutional policies and practices" that are to the advantage of Whites and the disadvantage of people of color" (7). Given this definition, Tatum wonders if people of color can be racist. Certainly bigotry can occur within any racial group—but can this behavior be considered racist? Tatum argues that it depends on one's definition of racism. If racism is defined as racial prejudice, certainly people of color can be just as racist as Whites. But if racism is defined as a system of advantage according to race, then the answer would have to be "no," because the system does not benefit people of color in any way.[2] The larger issue this question raises is that racism has definite benefits and costs depending on one's racial identity and point of view.

How Do We Learn About Race, Ethnicity, and Bias? Children first learn about race and racial bias from parents and teachers. It generally begins as young children reach the cognitive level at which they can discriminate among colors. It may begin, as Banton pointed out, with an innocent question: "Why are they not like us?" How a parent responds is the first key step in the process of racial identity formation. If the parent is uncomfortable, yanks the child away, or says something evasive like "We don't talk about that in public," the child begins to learn that there might be something wrong with people who are not the same color. In fact, they may be someone to be feared. On the other hand, if the child is given a metaphoric explanation—such as the one Helms relates, "Some people were left in God's oven longer than others"—a benchmark for what is "normal" is established (White), indicating that people of color are therefore abnormal, "burned," or somehow not wholesome (6). Similarly, an off-the-cuff remark such as "People can't help

Figure 2–2. "*Snooty Patooty, nose in the air, Snooty Patooty, just didn't care . . .*" *A scene about intolerance from* Cootie Shots *(Fringe Benefits Theatre Co.).* Photo by Norma Bowles.

what color they are" indicates that they just can't help not being like us (White) and are therefore to be pitied (6).

Prejudice begins with these preconceptions, judgments, and opinions based on partial information along with a tacit understanding of the advantage of Whiteness that is generally never overtly discussed. Imagine the confusion a young person might feel when the only real times Whiteness is mentioned is when a supremacist group or individual acts out. The unspoken rule is that Whiteness is not supposed to be consciously acknowledged unless one is a bigot—which is culturally unacceptable (Helms, 9). Young people are left with confusing messages about the relationship between their own racial and ethnic identities and the identities of "others."

As young people absorb their understanding of race, racial preference, and racism from adults, they also gather a good deal of information from the larger social systems that surround them. We cannot avoid developing a tacit understanding of the systems of oppression that permeate our schools, places of employment, and government. We learn at an early age that certain colors of people often labor at particular kinds of jobs, behave in particular kinds of ways, and possess particular kinds of skills or attributes while certain others do not. When we have direct experience with racial or ethnic others, there is a tendency to extrapolate from that experience and turn it into an emblematic moment—as if the total history and understanding of what it means to be Black, Native American, or Japanese somehow resides deep within this one person we've encountered. A college student once complained to me that, as the only Asian in a class on Asian dance, she repeatedly felt as if she was being asked to be the "poster child" for all things Asian. She resented the assumptions about her presumed cultural knowledge and subsequently dropped the class.

I experienced the awkwardness of being an emblematic White woman when I lived in India. Although I always dressed modestly in conservative *salwar kameez* pantsuits, many people assumed I embodied a host of preconceived notions about American women—including that we are all rich, selfish, sexually promiscuous and therefore immoral. At a provocative performance of vignettes about women's rights, my difference was made especially acute. "We don't want to be like Western women who have no respect for family," one Indian woman asserted during the postshow discussion. All eyes fell on me. "We don't want to be like them," the woman accused. How do you explain emblematic stereotyping across language and cultural gulfs? How can we help others "unlearn" deeply ingrained misperceptions?

Cultural forms such as drama and theatre work can also teach stereotypes and racial biases. For example, I once found myself perniciously "playing" at being Chinese in an improvisational drama led by a colleague from England that was ostensibly about China's "one child" policy. Participants were asked to interpret several artifacts—including a series of headlines and memos about national and local birth control efforts in China and a specific request for a second child that had been denied by the Public Security Bureau (PSB). We busily invented the specific circumstances that might have inspired the request and how the message from the PSB would be delivered and acted on. In the middle of the improvisation, however, I started asking myself: "Why am I hunched over, moving slowly, bowing unnecessarily, talking slowly and deliberately? Why am I rigid in attitude and projecting unfeelingness? *Why* am I playing stereotypes? Why am I being allowed to in this drama?"

During a wrap-up discussion I asked the drama leader how we could avoid rehearsing stereotypes in drama work of this nature. From his perspec-

Figure 2–3. *Fursey Gotuaco prepares a racially diverse group of students to see a performance of* I Remember Ernie *by Matt Buchanan (Produced by the University of Texas at Austin).* Photo by Amy Handler.

tive, our representations of the "Chinese" were only important insofar as they helped us deal with a "universal" element of the human condition—that of overpopulation. "This is not a drama about the Chinese or stereotyping. What we are dealing with here," he stated slowly and deliberately, "is the common plight of *all* humanity and what other options might there be as we try to keep the world in a holdable form." While this drama leader was on his way to larger supposedly "universal" understandings, a number of troubling stereotypes were reinforced about what it "means" to be Chinese. My concern is that young people learn about race and racial bias in a number of ways from adults, including through our drama and theatre work. Stereotyping about what a group of people is "really" like through uncritical imagined understandings of their values and experience merely perpetuates racial and ethnic bias. As teachers and practitioners, we need to pay closer attention to what we pass on as "cultural" truth in our work.

More than Good Intentions: Working Against Racial Bias. Helms notes that social psychologist James Jones articulates three typical forms of racism: individual, cultural, and institutional (17). Each can exist overtly or covertly. They can also be challenged overtly or covertly. On a personal level, one might avoid racially motivated jokes, spurn bigotry, or remind others that the lack of perceived success by a non-White person or group has nothing to do with genetic inferiority or laziness. However, one may overlook how cultural beliefs may reinforce racist doctrines through language superiority (English only) or lack of access to the political sphere. Specific institutions can have their own particularized brand of institutionalized racism: law enforcement agencies have the controversial policy of "racial profiling," the banking system has elaborate loan application review procedures for "minority" applicants, the education system "tracks" students into low-performing and special education classes that primarily consist of students of color. While well-meaning White liberals might desire to distance themselves from racial policies they do not agree with on a personal level, it is at the institutional level that racism persists and needs to be vigorously addressed.

Since Helms believes that racism was invented by Whites to benefit Whites, she asserts that if the system of exclusion and bias based on race is to change, White people need to make the following commitments: 1) decide to abandon racism, 2) observe ways in which racism is maintained in your environments, 3) learn the differences between the expression of racism and the expression of White culture, 4) discover what is positive about being White (14). She charges that developing a positive White identity based not on superiority but on valuing diversity is crucial if racism is to be abandoned.

This is particularly important for those of us who embrace the goals of multicultural education. We need to move beyond feelings of guilt and shame as well as examine the liberal impulse to benignly "do good." Instead, we need to take action from well-examined and informed positions. Sonia Nieto articulates the problem succinctly:

> An initial and quite understandable reaction of European American teachers and students is to feel guilty. Such a reaction, however, although probably serving an initial useful purpose, needs to be understood as only one step in the process of becoming multiculturally literate and empowered. If it remains at this level, guilt only immobilizes. (1992, 21)

Toward Culturally "Response-able" Teaching. It is time for those of us who work with young people to acknowledge and overcome our own discomfort about discussing race and work toward productive ways to act responsibly because of and despite it. This means not only recognizing our own racial and ethnic identities but also the racial and ethnic identities of the young people we serve. Gloria Ladson-Billings (1994) points out that many White teachers are often uncomfortable about acknowledging student differences—especially racial differences. Instead, she explains, "teachers make such statements as 'I don't really see color, I just see children' or 'I don't care if they're red, green, or polka dot, I just treat them all like children'" (31).

How can anyone working with a group of young people really fail to see color? The mental energy it takes to block out race, ethnicity, and how these identity locations shape cultural experience is enormous. This supposedly "color blind" stance typifies what Joyce King (1991) has called "dysconscious racism." King asserts that these "limited and distorted understandings . . . about inequity and cultural diversity" define dyconsciousness, which she sees as "an uncritical habit of mind (including perceptions, attitudes, assumptions, and beliefs) that justifies inequity and exploitation by accepting the existing order of things as a given" (134–5). An exchange I observed in a classroom helps illustrate this point:

> "Didn't we agree that you were going to finish this writing assignment before you got to draw? Why haven't you finished it? Why do you always do this? Go to the Content Mastery room and finish this work. Now!"[3] The child glares at the teacher who has been yelling at him and then slowly picks up his papers and notebook and leaves the classroom. The ethnographer in me records this moment: White teacher, Black student, conflict, mutual rage, empty "why" questions.
>
> The markers of power and race in the classroom are immediately obvious. While the majority of the students packed into this small portable sit in table groupings, four boys sit apart from the others. Dubbed the "L" brothers by several teachers (Lavon, Lionel, Lenny, Lazell), their desks are arranged around the teacher's table. These boys are Black. All the other students are Latina/o. The teacher is White and speaks fluent Spanish after living in Central America for several years. It was one of the "L" brothers who was sent out of the room.

The teacher is quite open about his frustrations with the students, many of whom frequently arrive late in the morning completely unprepared for the tasks associated with learning. He is especially frustrated about the progress of his Black students. In an interview with me about his challenges as a teacher, he is quite candid:

> So many of the kids bring in a lot from home! And when they have problems at home, they aren't ready to learn. I know [a lot of them] are getting up by themselves in the morning. Maybe somebody is yelling at them. Maybe somebody is using drugs in front of them. They come to school, but they're not ready to work. They're thinking of all the other things: they forgot their backpack, they don't have clean clothes, they don't have lunch

> money, they didn't eat breakfast. No one pumped them up to come to school and they're not ready to learn when they get here.

This teacher is honestly struggling to make sense of the problems he feels his students face and, in particular, his feelings of failure with the Black students who, he repeatedly reminds me, "live in the projects." Blaming parents (and, by extension, race?) conveniently displaces the problem of this teacher's imbedded attitudes about Blacks and achievement. However, from the overt labeling of the students ("the 'L' brothers") to the covert assumptions regarding their abilities and constant need for remedial help, these students are at the mercy of a system in which assumptions concerning their abilities have limited their potential. Ladson-Billings asserts that teachers like this one are not racist in the conventional sense (32). While they may not be blatantly denying students access to education because of race, they are not unconscious of the subtler workings of racial bias, or as Ladson-Billings says, of the reality that some children are privileged and others are not. "Their 'dysconsciousness' comes," she argues, "when they fail to challenge the status quo, when they accept the given as inevitable" (32).

What does this have to do with drama? Lorenzo Garcia (1997) points out that while teachers may be sympathetic to student diversity by infusing multiethnic content in their teaching, through folk tales, short stories, poetry, and plays, "they may not have a dynamic understanding of ethnic differences" (97). The status quo is never challenged in any meaningful way. Instead, the uncritical notion of "different but equal" is reinforced. This is illustrated through the use of another kind of "color blindness"—color-blind casting. However, there are implications beyond the simple desire "to be fair" as students are encouraged to play "traditional" roles across racial identities in "nontraditional" ways. Garcia elaborates:

> For example, the strategy of color-blindness, on the one hand, may offer drama/theatre teachers a mechanism with which to be fair, provide uniformity in instruction, and give equal treatment to every student. Yet on the other hand, color-blindness may obscure the uniqueness of that individual's experiences, and by applying some universal standard (e.g., "artistic excellence") teachers may not gain sufficient information upon which to further define that student's educational needs and curricular choices. (97)

Garcia insists that understanding student differences goes beyond simply acknowledging that differences exist. By incorporating a more complex understanding of the educational process as both multicultural *and* social reconstructionist, Garcia argues, teachers can "direct the focus of the curriculum on social justice issues, problem solving, social critique, identity issues, citizen participation, empowerment, and making social changes" (98).

Following Garcia's reworking of Cynthia Dillard's provocative term, I submit that drama teachers and theatre practitioners need to be hyperaware of our "response-abilities" to students whose race and ethnicity may be different from our own (Dillard, quoted in Garcia 1999b). Garcia believes that we all need to be encouraged to develop our "response-able" capacities so we can carefully examine the images we hold about ourselves and one another as we strive to create classroom environments and performative events that honor diversity (1999a).

Building Awareness

The following lesson plans actively involve young people in conversations about race and ethnicity. Younger elementary students openly consider color as an identity marker in a dramatic situation based on the picture book *The Colors of Us.* Students at the upper elementary range question the roots of racial tension as they become involved with a group of neighbors who are in conflict. As is the case with all the lesson plans scattered throughout the book, I have made a distinction between instructional information and *teacher voice* by italicizing any direct questions or comments a teacher or drama leader might actually say to the participants. For more information about this style of planning, particular drama techniques used, or pedagogical rationale, please see the appendix.

TOPIC: RACE AND ETHNICITY—PHYSICAL CHARACTERISTICS

Focus **What makes us each uniquely different and special?**

Teaching Objectives

To create a positive environment in which to discuss the uniqueness of each person's physical characteristics;

To explore how skin color makes each person particularly unique and special;

To reflect on how we can work to dispel thepreconception that one set of physical characteristics is better than another.

Target Age K-3rd grade

Time Needed Two or three 45-minute periods

Materials

- A collage of people from different racial and ethnic backgrounds prepared before class.

- *The Colors of Us* by Karen Katz (New York: Henry Holt and Co., 1999). When seven-year-old Lena wants to paint a picture of herself using brown paint, her mother takes her on a walk through their neighborhood and helps her see that brown comes in many different shades.
- Crayons, markers, art paper. Materials for framing and hanging student work.
- Magazines, newspapers, other print materials with images of different ethnic and racial groups; glue, art paper.

Procedure

1. ENGAGE the students: Begin by asking the students to think of some of their favorite things (such as toys, food, pets, etc.). *What are some of the colors of those things? How many colors can we name?* Make a list. *The world is certainly a very colorful place. Not only are things colorful, but people are, too.* (Show the collage and see how many colors of people students can name. Encourage them to think about different shades of white, brown, black, etc.) *Today we are going to meet a girl named Lena who wants to paint a picture of herself. She, too, has become very interested in the different colors of people. Let's see what happens.*
2. SHARE the story: Gather children so everyone can see the pictures as the story unfolds. Ask the students about the various details in each picture, including the colors on each page, and how they might describe the colors of the people Lena meets in the story.
3. EXPLORE the story:

   a. Cooperative game: Ask the students to gather their chairs in a circle or to sit on a designated spot on the floor. (I often use colored tape to designate a drama circle with an X for each child on the floor.) *Everyone has things about themselves that are similar and things that are different from other people. Let's see if we can find out what some of those things are.* Have the students sit in a circle or stand on their spot for a few rounds of The Winds Are Blowing. The teacher/leader stands in the middle and says, "The winds are blowing for . . ." and completes the sentence with either a physical characteristic (brown hair), what someone is wearing (purple socks), likes or dislikes (pizza, spinach, etc.). When the statement is made, all those with that characteristic must change places. At the same time the person in the middle is also trying to get a spot. Whoever does not get a spot goes to the center and the game begins again. With young or shy children it can be useful to ask them to take one minute to think of two things they might say if they were in the middle. Sidecoach as needed with ideas: clothing, shoes, jewelry, hair color, eye color, skin color, favorite ice cream, favorite color, favorite TV show, and so on. If possible, encourage students to use colorful descriptive language with the characteristics they call out (people with cinnamon-colored skin, sunshine-colored hair, etc.).

b. Teacher in role: Tell the students that, in just a moment, you are going to become a different person. This person is going to ask them to do something very important. Pull up a chair and explain that as soon as you sit down the drama will start.

"*I'm thrilled that so many of you saw my poster calling for talented artists. Thank you for coming to this meeting about the upcoming art show. That is why you are here, isn't it? Well, of course it is! You certainly look like a talented bunch, too! I'm sure you are wondering about the art show. Let me tell you about it. It's called 'The Colors of Us.' Do you like it? I thought you would. I actually got the idea from a book I read that really excited me. This show will also be the grand opening of my new gallery. I want to make sure we include images of all the different people that make up our community. I'm not quite sure how to do that, though. Do you have any suggestions?* (Engage the students in brainstorming about including the various people that make up a community and about shades of skin color like the ones listed in the picture book. Use the picture book as a reference if you need to prompt them. Write down their suggestions.) *What images and colors do we need? How will we organize ourselves so we get a full range of those images and colors? Should we do collages or a mural or individual work?* (Use the collage as a prompt for further discussion. Encourage the students to begin to organize themselves into task groups. If possible, let the students decide how to proceed.) *Terrific! So, everyone knows what they need to do? Well then, let's meet back here tomorrow and see what you've come up with.*

c. Discuss: Out of role, clarify what the students need to do. Work to create an atmosphere in which it is safe and acceptable to look at and talk about skin color. Prompt students to find new and interesting ways to describe the different colors of skin.

d. Art work: Depending on the students and time available, do one or more of the following:

   1. Have students work in small groups to create a collage representing people from different racial and ethnic groupings.

2. Have students work independently or in small groups to create pictures of people with various shades of skin color. Challenge students to find "colorful" descriptive words for their pictures.
3. Have students create a mural on a large piece of butcher paper that shows all the different colors of people in their community.

e. Teacher in role/Students in role: Tell the students that it is time to show the gallery owner their work. Challenge them to consider: How will they present it? Who will talk about it? How will they discuss why the artwork is important to them?

"*Hello, everybody! I can't tell you how much I've been looking forward to seeing you all again. Let's get right to it. Who wants to start?*"

Encourage the group to boldly share their work and insights. Thank them for their hard work and make plans for the gallery opening. (This could coincide with an open house or an invitation to another class to come and see their work.)

4. REFLECT on the issues: *Sometimes it's awkward for people to talk about skin color. Why do you suppose that is? What is it about skin color that seems to upset some people? What would you want to tell people who are uncomfortable talking about this?*
5. EVALUATE the lesson: What did you notice about the group's willingness to discuss this issue? Was there any reluctance to engage? If so, why? What stereotypes were brought up? How do you feel you handled them? How did the students portray people from different racial backgrounds? What things still need to be examined? What questions did you have trouble answering? Which discussion segments worked best? Why? What do students seem most interested in concerning this issue? Based on your evaluation, how might you follow up this lesson?

Possible Extensions

Language Arts

Create a poster for the upcoming art show at the gallery. Depending on the grade level, write a review of the show.

Create a personal narrative to accompany each picture.

Art

How do galleries let people know about upcoming shows? Examine promotional material from various local galleries. Take a field trip to see how art galleries display artwork.

How have other artists tried to represent the "colors of us" in different ways? Examine the artwork of several different artists from different cultural backgrounds.

Social Studies

Who are all the people who make up our community? Make a list of the various racial and ethnic groups in your community. If useful, map where different people live or where significant landmarks are to honor these various groups.

TOPIC: RACE AND ETHNICITY—TENSIONS BETWEEN PEOPLE

Focus How can tensions between different communities be resolved?

Teaching Objectives

To discuss racial and ethnic stereotypes and preconceptions;

To explore the issues and challenges those stereotypes may cause between different groups of people;

To reflect on how we can work to help resolve tensions caused by misperceptions.

Target Age 4th–6th grade

Time Needed Two 45-minute sessions

Materials

- A rock with a note tied to it. Scrawled on the note is the phrase "Go back to where you came from."
- *Smoky Night* by Eve Bunting (San Diego, CA: Harcourt Brace and Co., 1994). When racial tensions lead to a riot in the streets of their neighborhood, a boy and his mother learn to appreciate others regardless of their backgrounds.

Procedure

1. ENGAGE the students: Ask students to examine the rock and read the note. Explain that a rock like this was thrown through a window by someone who was very angry. (You may need to reiterate that this is not the "real" rock that was thrown but having it here as a symbol might help us understand more about why some people behave the

way they do.) *Why might someone be that angry? Who might they be angry with? Why would they resort to throwing a rock through someone's window? These are very hard questions. Today we are going to try to understand why tensions exist between different kinds of people and wonder if there is anything we can do to help ease those tensions.*

2. SHARE part of the story: Gather the students and read *Smoky Night* up to and including page five, which describes a man taking a pile of clothes from a dry cleaning shop. (Although the whole book will not be shared with the class at this point, it can be finished at the end of the lesson.) Ask: *I wonder why these people might be acting this way?* List the students' ideas on the chalkboard, flip chart, or overhead. Ask: *I wonder what kinds of feelings this kind of event evokes.* List the students' ideas. *Let's try to get a better idea about what's going on here.*
3. EXPLORE the story:
    a. Group emotion: Begin by examining some of the feelings people might have about a situation like this. Ask for one volunteer to stand in the center of the playing area. The teacher or leader gives the volunteer an emotion or state of being from the list generated during brainstorming and asks them to physicalize the emotion or feeling as a frozen image. Ask half of the remaining students to one at a time place themselves in the image in a way that also expresses something about the emotion in relation to the first pose. When everyone is in place, the leader slowly counts from one to five as the players to intensify the emotion in slow motion. At "five," they freeze once more. The observers are asked to describe what they see and comment on what the picture might have to do with the riot. Repeat the exercise with the other half of the class. Try to choose contrasting emotions such as rage and fear. Ask the class about the similarities and differences between these two emotions.
    b. Scene development: Students will now look back at the history of the neighborhood and the different people in it to see how this riot might have started. *We will look at some different moments and see how these conflicts might have developed. We will first look at the seed of this conflict at Kim's Market one year ago. We'll then watch how the conflict grew at Morton's Appliances six months ago. We'll also see what happened at the dry cleaner's a week ago and at Fashion Shoes one hour before this riot broke out.*

        Divide the students into four groups. Give each group a slip of paper explaining the situation they will be exploring and a possible incident. *Your job as a group is to create a scene in which there is conflict between at least two people over this incident. Keep in the back of your mind that we are looking at the history of the riot, and watching it build.* Give each group a slip of paper with the following information:

Group 1—Kim's Market: one year prior to the riot. A leaflet stuck on the door handle that says, "We buy from our own kind."

Group 2—Morton's Appliances: six months prior to the riot. A hate group poster taped to the window.

Group 3—Dry cleaners: one week prior to the riot. Blood poured on the steps outside the front door.

Group 4—Fashion Shoes: one hour prior to the riot. A rock with a note smashes through the front window.

c. Share scenes: Have the groups share their scenes one at a time. After each scene, discuss the characters, situation, attitudes about others, and where these attitudes might come from. *How do people learn these attitudes?* After all of the scenes have been played, ask the group to consider how the people in each of these scenes might have avoided this conflict. *What could have happened differently?* (Discuss in depth or, for advanced groups, proceed to the next exercise.)

d. Replay one scene: Ask one group to volunteer to share their scene again. *Let's watch the scene again, but this time we will attempt to find ways the conflict might have been avoided. As you watch the scene, look for something one of the characters could do differently that might change the outcome. If you have an idea, yell "Freeze," and the actors will stop the scene. You can then replace one of the actors and try out your idea. I may stop you after a while and ask the group if your action changed the situation or not and see if anyone has any other ideas.* Evaluate each intervention: *What did the protagonist want? Did the situation change? How? If it did not change, what was the problem? How else might the characters get what they want?*

4. REFLECT on the issues: *What causes tensions between different racial and ethnic groups? What do stereotypes and misperceptions about different people have to do with it? What can we do to help get rid of these kinds of tensions?*

5. EVALUATE the lesson: What did you notice about the group's willingness to discuss this issue? Was there any reluctance to engage? If so, why? What stereotypes were brought up? How do you feel you handled

them? How did the students portray people from different racial backgrounds? What things still need to be examined? What questions did you have trouble answering? Which discussion segments worked best? Why? What do students seem most interested in concerning this issue? Based on your evaluation, how might you follow up this lesson?

Possible Extensions

Language Arts

Write a story about the scene you were working on. How might you change peoples' attitudes and avoid the riot?

Social Studies

This story is about the riots in Los Angeles in 1992. Have students research and discuss what led up to those riots.

Examine periods of history when riots have erupted over race or ethnicity. What could have been done to prevent them? Have students create a story, a play, or a series of drawings to test your idea.

Health

Look at ways various ways people can effectively resolve conflicts. Have students create a poster to help remind people how to deal with conflict situations.

Creating an Environment for Equity

There are many ways to add an awareness of racial and ethnic diversity to your teaching. While content choices are extremely important, developing the critical thinking skills necessary to analyze content and the relevant issues raised is vital. Below I have synthesized several strategies drama and theatre practitioners might find useful.

James Banks (1999) has identified five dimensions of multicultural education (14). These include:

- content integration
- knowledge construction
- prejudice reduction
- equity pedagogy
- an empowering classroom culture and structure

Of these, three are particularly useful for drama teachers and theatre practitioners. Under the umbrella of "knowledge construction," there are several active strategies for creating an awareness of race and ethnicity:

- Give students the opportunity to explore likenesses and differences in depth.
- Make sure material in question is appropriate for cognitive development level.
- Create a stimulating environment that exposes young people to a range of diversity.
- Lead discussions and inquiry through questioning, not lecturing.

Similarly, "prejudice reduction" can be addressed in the drama classroom and in theatrical productions in the following ways:

- Prefer teaching materials that are free of stereotypes.
- If stereotypes occur, examine misconceptions openly and directly.
- Create an environment that is not color blind.
- Model positive attitudes about diversity.
- Create an atmosphere that inspires respect and tolerance.

Added to this list is Bank's regard for "equity pedagogy," which, as Robles de Meléndez and Ostertag (1997) argue, prompts educators to ask several questions about their teaching. These questions can also be asked about the drama and theatre work we undertake with any group:

- Are all children treated equally?
- Are all children offered a sense of success?
- Do I show to every child that I believe in what he/she can do?
- Do I adapt/change the curriculum for the child?
- Do I show children that I respect and value their cultural identities?

Despite our best efforts, ingrained attitudes about others are sometimes hard for students to abandon. Banks (1999) offers some specific guidelines for reducing prejudice in students based on his research:

1. Include positive and realistic images of ethnic and racial groups in teaching materials in a consistent, natural, and integrated fashion.
2. Help children to differentiate the faces of members of outside racial and ethnic groups.

3. Involve children in vicarious experiences with various racial and ethnic groups. (This could include videos, children's books, drama and theatre work, and so on.)
4. If you teach in an interracial school, involve children in structured interracial contact situations.
5. Provide positive verbal and nonverbal reinforcement for the color brown.
6. Involve children from different racial and ethnic groups in cooperative learning activities. (48)

Many drama and theatre teachers and practitioners worry about the tensions that might exist between various communities of students which, in turn, might negatively affect their ability to work together on creative projects. Allport (quoted in Banks 1999, 47) suggests that prejudice can be reduced in interracial contact situations if the meetings are

> *cooperative* rather than competitive encounters in which all individuals feel they have *equal status* and the *same goals*. It also helps if the work is *sanctioned* by parents and upper administration.

The benefit of struggling with these difficult issues is the hope of expanding the ways in which students think about race, ethnicity, themselves, and others. Louise Derman-Sparks (1989) suggests several admirable goals for an antibiased curriculum. In her work as in ours, every child should be able to

- construct a knowledgeable, confident self-identity;
- develop comfortable, empathetic, and just interaction with diversity;
- develop critical thinking skills;
- develop the skills for standing up for oneself and others in the face of injustice. (ix)

Based on my own struggles with creating an ongoing awareness of race and ethnicity in my teaching and creative work, I offer the following suggestions:

- Be aware of the messages you send with the comments you make in front of young people.
- Strive for language that is inclusive and that respects diversity.
- Do not forget the impact your attitude toward diversity has on your students. Your positive attitude about your own racial identity will help foster positive feelings about your students' identities.
- Pick diversity-rich source materials for lessons or performance events.

- Do not assume that monocultural groups have no need to deal with diversity. Help them embrace and understand their own and other racial and ethnic identity positions.
- Remember to incorporate a variety of instructional strategies to meet the needs of your various learners (verbal, visual, kinesthetic, aural, etc.).
- Remember that space matters in terms of seating or working arrangements as well as what is in your room: books, posters on the walls, music, bulletin boards, and so on. How can your space reflect a commitment to racial and ethnic diversity?
- Embrace language diversity and have the presence of other languages in your room and your work.
- Don't be afraid to face the issues when they come up!

Lastly, in *Making Meaning of Whiteness*, Alice McIntyre (1997) suggests the following:

> One strategy for becoming more critical about multicultural education as antiracist education is for white teachers to be more self-reflective about our own understandings about race and racism and for us to challenge our own construction about what it means to be white in this country. How do we, as white teachers, become more self-reflective? How do we learn to acknowledge our own sense of ourselves as racial beings actively participating in the education of young people? How do we become multicultural antiracist people? (14)

The questions and practical problems listed below help address McIntyre's concerns and are designed to promote reflective practice.

Questions to Ponder

1. Consider your own racial and ethnic identity locations. How would you situate yourself in relationship to race? How would you describe your ethnicity? When did you first become aware of these identity locations? What incidents or relationships have caused you to notice your identity positions?
2. How would you describe the racial and ethnic positions of the students you ordinarily work with? What tensions does race or ethnicity cause between students? How do *your* race and ethnic positions affect your work with these students? What incidents have caused you to notice

these tensions? What might be the role of racial bias in these situations? What can you do to alleviate these tensions?

3. How would you categorize the racial and ethnic backgrounds of peers in your working environment? How do these racial and ethnic positions affect relationships between peers? What is the role of bias in these relationships? What can you do about it?
4. There is great political debate over the degree to which racial categories should be considered in policies concerning affirmative action, immigration, welfare, and access to education. What do you think? Should economic circumstances be more of a determinant than race? Can access to economic success be separated from racial identity? What does this begin to suggest about the relationship between race and privilege?
5. Geneva Gay (1997, 213) has asked, "How can teachers who have grown up in ethnically isolated communities and in a racist society teach students whom they do not know, may not value, and may even fear?" How would you address her question?

Practical Problems to Consider

1. Working with a retelling of the Pocahontas legend as a source for creative drama or theatre work, how would you structure the work so that racial bias was fully examined?
2. You are working with a group of Latina/o second graders on a drama about building an imaginary community. During part of the improvisation work, one student announces that no other racial group should be allowed to join their new community. How do you respond?
3. When working with a multiaged mixed-race group in an afterschool program, you notice that the students always self-select into race-based groupings. They object strongly when asked to work with others outside their racial group. How do you talk about the problem with them?
4. A fourth-grade colleague has asked you to help him plan a drama-based unit on Japanese American culture as part of a larger unit on immigration. How might you create an activity or lesson that includes an understanding that racial identity is always negotiated relative to context?
5. A group of colleagues has decided to create a series of initiatives to help encourage awareness of racial bias in your organization and has asked you for some advice. What would you suggest? How would you counsel them to progress from awareness to action?

A Case Study Situation

It is Black History Month and your school district is centering this year's celebration on Martin Luther King's "I Have a Dream" speech. Your group has been asked to create a performance that can tour to fifteen schools throughout the district during the month of February. The company currently consists of a White director, a Latina business manager, and four actors (three White and one Latino). Money is tight. You could hire another actor *or* commission a designer to create a provocative touring set—but you can not do both. How do you proceed? How do you justify your decisions? What kind of performance will you create for this event given your decisions? How do understandings of race, ethnicity, and privilege enter into your process?

Resources for Drama and Theatre Work on Race and Ethnicity

The following books represent only a few of the many resources currently on the market that feature ethnically diverse protagonists. They each have lots of potential for exploration through drama!

Picture Books

African American

The Leaving Morning by Angela Johnson (New York: Orchard Books, 1992). On moving day, a young man says goodbye to his neighborhood, friends, and apartment.

Tar Beach by Faith Ringgold (New York: Crown Publishers, 1991). A young girl imagines she can fly over her Harlem neighborhood.

Your Move by Eve Bunting (San Diego, CA: Harcourt Brace, 1998). A gang initiation threatens the life of a young boy's brother.

Biracial

A Visit to Amy-Claire by Claudia Mills (New York: Macmillan, 1992). A trip to a cousin's house causes tension between two sisters.

Billy and Belle by Sarah Garland (New York: Viking Penguin, 1992). On the day their new brother is to be born, young Belle goes to school with Billy and accidentally releases all the animals brought in for Pet Day.

How My Parents Learned to Eat by Ina R. Friedman (Boston, MA: Houghton Mifflin, 1984). An American soldier and a Japanese woman learn about each others' cultural customs.

Japanese American

Baseball Saved Us by Ken Mochizuki (New York: Lee and Low Books, 1993). When his family is forced into an internment camp, a young boy learns to play baseball.

El Chino by Allen Say (Boston, MA: Houghton Mifflin, 1990). A Chinese American boy grows up to be a bullfighter in Spain.

The Journey by Sheila Hamanaka (New York: Orchard Books, 1990). A mural provides a backdrop for the history of Japanese immigrants in America.

Latina/o

Family Pictures/Cuadros de familia by Carmen Lomas Garza (San Francisco, CA: Children's Book Press, 1990). Contains several short bilingual stories about growing up in a Latina/o community in Texas.

Santiago by Pura Belpre (New York: Frederick Warne and Co., 1969). A young Puerto Rican misses his country and his pet hen as he tries to adjust to his new surroundings.

Taking Sides by Gary Soto (San Diego, CA: Harcourt Brace, 1991). A move from the inner city to a White suburb causes a young man to struggle with divided loyalties.

American Indian

Less Than Half, More Than Whole by Kathleen and Michael Lacapa (Flagstaff, AZ: Northland Publishing, 1994). A young boy is troubled by his mixed racial heritage.

The People Shall Continue by Simon Ortiz (San Francisco, CA: Children's Book Press, 1988). A historical account of American Indians from the creation to the present.

Plays

North Star by Gloria Bond Clunie (available from Dramatic Publishing at 203-254-6624 or e-mail: <dramaticpb@aol.com>). An African American girl becomes involved in the struggle for civil rights in the 1960s.

Amazing Grace by Shay Youngblood, adapted from the book by Mary Hoffman (available from Dramatic Publishing at 203-254-6624 or e-mail: <dramaticpb@aol.com>.) Tensions erupt when a highly creative girl is told she cannot play Peter Pan in the class play because she is a girl and she is Black.

Bocon! by Lisa Loomer (in C. Jennings' *Theatre for Young Audiences: 20 Great Plays for Children,* New York: St. Martin's Press, 1998). A boy from Central America flees his homeland and struggles to reach the borderlands toward his hope for freedom.

Five Good Resources on Race and Ethnicity

Helms, J. E. 1992. *A Race Is a Nice Thing to Have: A Guide to Being a White Person or Understanding the White Persons in Your Life.* Topeka, KS: Content Communications. A short, no-nonsense analysis of the mechanics of racism and what it takes to develop a positive White identity.

Jacobson, M. F. 1998. *Whiteness of a Different Color: European Immigrants and the Alchemy of Race.* Cambridge, MA: Harvard University Press. A compelling study of the invention of White identity and the historical changeability of racial categories.

Mathias, B. and M. A. French.1996. *40 Ways to Raise a Non-racist Child.* New York: HarperCollins. Although geared toward families, this book is full of useful ways to openly talk about racism with young people.

McIntyre, A. 1997. *Making Meaning of Whiteness: Exploring Racial Identity with White Teachers.* Albany, NY: State University of New York Press. A group of White teachers examines their understandings of "Whiteness" and consider how they might work to eliminate White privilege from the experience of school.

Tatum, B. D. 1999. *"Why Are All the Black Kids Sitting Together in the Cafeteria?" and Other Conversations About Race.* New York: Basic Books. A frank and compelling examination of the persistence of racial barriers and what educators can do to intervene.

Notes

1. Jacobson (1998) persuasively argues that the presumption of Anglo-Saxon privilege forced a rethinking of race as various ethnic minorities (Irish and Greeks, for example) were "reracialized" to become Caucasian.

2. For a further discussion of this point see Beverly Daniel Tatum (1999), Chapter 1.

3. In this school, a team of three Content Mastery teachers provides one-on-one tutoring and additional learning support for students in need of extra help with assignments.

4.This lesson plan is adapted from an idea presented by students Regina Arzamendi and Lynn Hoare in my creative drama class at the University of Texas in the fall of 1995.

3

Class-Oriented Locations

the "intense silence"

"[N]owhere is there a more intense silence about the reality of class differences than in educational settings."

—BELL HOOKS, *TEACHING TO TRANSGRESS*

It's been a miserable day. And it's becoming an equally miserable evening—a soggy, cold April evening of camping out for a group of fifth-grade students I've been doing drama with for the semester. We've hiked. We've done several quasi-scientific experiments. We've played theatre games. We've eaten hot dogs. And we've just finished ghost stories around the campfire. The eight street-savvy girls in my cabin are genuinely frightened here in the woods—a context completely unfamiliar to them. They are particularly terrified of *La Llorona,* they tell me, the ghostly woman of legend who drowned her own children and haunts the land looking for others to terrorize. At every sound they consider odd (numerous in this creaky cabin) they scream and jump onto my bunk. We are all cold and trying to make the best of it, but some of the girls don't have sleeping bags or coats. And the weather is getting worse.

I ask one of the teachers in the next cabin to look after my girls while I go in search of something, anything, to keep these kids warm. In the dining hall I run into the principal, a woman of considerable energy, who has already anticipated the problem and has called for extra supplies to be delivered. While we wait, I begin to express my frustration over the girls' needs and, unexpectedly, it *all* comes pouring out—the problems during the semester with discipline, the tensions between students, the way teachers and students treat each other, the pervasive sense of hopelessness in this school that is 77 percent Latina/o, 21 percent Black, and 2 percent White.

"Look, it isn't really about race. It's about poverty," she says putting a hand on my arm. "It's about dealing with lack. It affects everything you and they do together. Think about it."

I don't want to believe her. I want to locate the trouble in ethnicity and the clash of racial differences and the resulting student (and teacher) intolerance. After all, I knew my White skin was a passport that allowed me to traverse the racial divide in our city with ease. Interstate 35 clearly inscribes the racial and economic geography by separating the solidly middle- and upper-middle-class West side (which is mostly White) from the impoverished East side (which is mostly inhabited by people of color). But those words haunt: "It's about dealing with lack." While a disproportionate number of people of color also occupy poor or working social class positions, how often does the complexity and discomfort of racial politics obscure attention to the conflicts that exist between social class positions and the relative power struggles that result? Perhaps more *is* going on here.

ABC's of Social Class

Curiously, the reality of differing social class positions is downplayed in the United States. As bell hooks (1994) has noted, when it comes to education, social class differences are simply not discussed. She elaborates:

> From grade school on, we are all encouraged to cross the threshold of the classroom believing we are entering a democratic space—a free zone where the desire to study and learn makes us all equal. And even if we enter accepting the reality of class differences, most of us still believe knowledge will be meted out in fair and equal proportions." (177)

If social class is acknowledged at all, which it is usually only at the lower end, it is often cloaked in euphemisms such as "economically deprived" or "economically disadvantaged" which, of course, marks students as "at risk." This language of "cultural deficiency" is shaped in opposition to the dominant culture's sense of entitlement, access, and achievement, which views nondominant members as somehow "lacking" on many levels (Sleeter 1996, 44–5).

In this chapter, I want to consider class as a site of difference in general and analyze its impact on drama and theatre in education work in particular. I will outline the various cultures that evolve around class standing and consider the middle-class values and codes around which various social institutions such as school (and mainstream theatre) are based (Payne 1995, 8). I will also attempt to unknot the differences between class and race and examine the connection between class and power. Lastly, I will consider how these understandings of social class affect us as theatre workers or teachers who desire to teach and create in culturally relevant and inclusive ways.

In order to build a greater awareness of class-related issues, the two lesson plans included in this chapter encourage students to consider both a fanciful situation about a king and his subjects as well as an all-too-real situation concerning homelessness. In the final part of the chapter, I discuss several ways to create a more equitable learning environment that acknowledges social class.

Analyzing Social Class

In a recent discussion about how social class affects the arts, a British friend noted, "You Americans don't talk much about class, do you?" No, we don't. Why? One theory is that class identity has been virtually stripped from our popular culture, and therefore from our collective imagination. Gregory Mantsios (1998) observes two exceptions: first, the pervasive generic references to "the middle class," which we are all assumed to be, conveniently glosses over differences and avoids any suggestion of conflict or exploitation; second, glimpses of the extremes, that is, the upper-class life of wealth (as in *Lifestyles of Rich and Famous*) or lower-class life of poverty (those "real cops" shows with real down-and-out underclass criminals), both of which obscure the reality of class differences and their impact on people's lives (203). For purposes of this discussion, I will refer to the following four social class positions: poor, working-class, middle-class, and wealthy.

It is often difficult to separate class from racial identity. While it is true that a disproportionate number of people of color are also poor and working-class, there is no inherent determining connection between the two. In fact, as Mary Fuller (1996) points out, upper-middle-class Black students have more in common with upper-middle-class White students than with Black students from federally subsidized housing projects (144). Recent debates concerning affirmative action have posited that social class is a more compelling indicator of lack of access and need than race or ethnicity. While group membership in nondominant racial and ethnic categories still bars access to equal opportunity in this country, class standing has a significant impact on chances for educational and economic attainment.

Further, social class and economic advantage directly affects the amount of money spent per student in school districts and is therefore linked to the quality of education a student receives or the additional education services available. Since the initial money schools receive is based on the property taxes collected from community members, the primary reason for school inequality is social class.[1] In *Savage Inequalities*, education critic Jonathan Kozol (1991) points out that even after years of court disputes and state formula revisions, spending per pupil in Texas ranges from $2,000 in the poorest districts to $19,000 in the richest (223).

Class standing, and consequently life chances, are largely determined at birth, Mantsios asserts. Although examples of individuals who have gone from rags to riches abound in mass media, statistics on class mobility show these leaps to be extremely rare. For those with six-figure annual incomes, economic success is due in large part to the wealth and privileges bestowed on them at birth (211). Despite the rhetoric, all Americans *do not* have an equal opportunity to succeed.

My Early Education in Class Relations. The first time I realized we might be poor was when a well-meaning lady at the Southern Baptist church my mother made us go to gave me a bag of clothes. "Here, my dear. These are for you," she said as she handed me a worn shopping bag. "My daughter has outgrown them. I thought that you might be able to use them." There was an awkward silence as I stared at the bag and then at her.

"Thanks," I said with a forced smile, because I knew that was the expected response. I took the bag and immediately turned away, muttering a few very un-Christian things under my breath. My twelve-year-old face was on fire. I quickly looked around wondering if anyone had seen this interaction. On the way home I threw the bag away—and vowed I'd work harder to keep our "situation" our secret.

A divorce had plunged us into an alternate economic reality requiring a quick series of survival moves on my mother's part. My mother was British and had married young, had little education, and few marketable skills. She immediately had to deal with citizenship, learn how to drive a car, and find an adequate job. We were poor—another statistic in what came to be defined as the "working-poor," although I didn't really understand it at the time. At first glance, our predicament would appear to have been situational. In retrospect, however, I wonder if it was more connected to generational poverty, that is, poverty that has affected at least two generations or more (Payne 1995, 7). My sketchy understanding of my mother's family history was that they were used to scraping by. For several generations they had been poor laborers from East Anglia—the fen country made theatrically famous by Caryl Churchill. *They* were poor, but this was America. How could we possibly be poor enough for church charity?

From an adult perspective, I can understand more clearly that poverty is often masked—not easily recognizable. Political scientist Michael Harrington (1962) has commented, "America has the best-dressed poverty the world has ever known." Clothing disguises much of the poverty in the U.S., which helps explain the prevailing assumption of middle-classness. Most middle-class Americans don't ever really see poverty. If they do, it's a kind of touristic siting—on the way to the airport, on the way to a trendy new little gallery, on the way out of town, on the way to somewhere else. But the poor see *them.* In 1903, W. E. B. Du Bois observed that African Americans hold a "double consciousness"—their own and White people's. Similarly the poor are very aware of those who are not.

Each social class position has definitive attitudes about those who occupy the other ranks. For example, in her essay "Stupidly 'Deconstructed'," Joanne Kadi (1996) relates a series of incidents in which she was made aware of the construction of class attitudes. Born in a working-class Lebanese American family, Kadi says she learned at an early age that workers are "stupid" and executives are "smart." She writes:

> This didn't happen because of a weird personal quirk. It resulted from force-fed images and words of TV shows, newspapers, magazines, and movies. Any TV show with working-class characters, first "The Honeymooners" and "I Love Lucy," then "All in the Family," covertly and overtly highlighted the stupidity of bus drivers, factory workers, and plumbers. Movies, books, and comic followed suit. At school, middle-class kids called us "stupid;" we hurled back "stuck up," but never "stupid." Working-class/working-poor kids failed and dropped out, but not middle-class kids. Our town newspaper consistently portrayed General Motors executives as calm, rational types, while union members appeared unthinking, wild, and chaotic. (48)

These kinds of attitudes and assumptions are played out in educational institutions in various ways. The practice of tracking, for example, has been criticized for segregating students along color and class lines under the pretense of assessing and responding to ability. A majority of the middle-class and upper-middle-class students end up in the highest-ability groupings while working-class or working-poor students end up in the low-performing groups. Young people are not oblivious to this game and learn early on how preferential treatment operates. Although they may not be able to articulate it clearly, they know they are different (and less than) for some reason others have determined.

The Construction of Class. Class, like race and gender, is a social construct. These culturally constructed differences "reflect and perpetuate the prevailing distribution of power and privilege in society." (Rothenberg 1998, 8) As with all identity coordinates, the complex set of traits and beliefs that map our material reality, class, race, and gender are in messy and overlapping relation to one another. Gender and racial oppression cuts across class lines. Class oppression permeates other spheres of power and oppression, so that the oppression experienced, for example, by women and people of color is also differentiated along class lines (Mantsios 1998, 212). Class-oppressed men (Black or White) have special privileges in a sexist society. Class-oppressed Whites (men or women) have privileges as Whites in a racist society. Likewise Black middle-class youth have more privileges than poor or working-class youth (Black or White).

The Codes of Social Class: A Beginning Understanding. Although I am highly suspicious of fast-and-loose-generalizations about any identity coordinate, there are patterns that occur with great regularity and affect the material conditions of real people when access to economic capital is limited. In her book *Poverty: A Framework for Understanding and Working with Students and Adults from Poverty* (1995) Ruby Payne articulates several key observations about social class from her vantage point as a former principal in both wealthy and materially impoverished schools. According to Payne, we all bring with us the "hidden rules" of the class culture in which we are raised, and although our economic circumstances may change significantly, our class-based patterns of thought, social interaction, and cognitive strategies remain intact (8). For example, in my own experience of growing up in a working-poor environment, I learned to indulge when I had money because tomorrow I might not. Saving and planning was not something that I was taught to value. Now, as an upper-middle-class adult, I frustrate my partner when I immediately spend an unexpected reimbursement check or tax refund as a result of this ingrained pattern.

While Payne acknowledges that all trends have exceptions, she offers a quiz as an introduction to the hidden rules of class and their relationship to basic survival (83–89). I have excerpted a few of these quiz questions in Figure 3–1. The point of this test is to reiterate that, regardless of class status, knowledge of the "rules" often associated with a specific class position is taken for granted. Specifically, Payne asserts that the middle-class norms and hidden rules by which most social institutions operate are presumably transparent and therefore are never directly taught (8). For all students to have an even chance of surviving the institution of school, she believes educators must understand these hidden rules and teach students the rules that will make them successful at both school and work (9). By practicing the "Teaching the Culturally Different Approach" to multicultural education identified by Sleater and Grant (1994), some educators have tried to redress this situation by stressing relevant social and academic skills. This assimilationist tactic provides

A QUIZ: HOW WELL DO YOU KNOW THE HIDDEN RULES OF CLASS?

Could you survive in poverty?

(Put a check beside the items you have experienced or know how to do.)

_____ 1. I know which churches and sections of town have the best rummage sales.

_____ 2. I know which grocery stores' garbage bins can be accessed for thrown away food.

_____ 3. I know how to keep my clothes from being stolen at the laundromat.

_____ 4. I know how to live without a checking account.

_____ 5. I know where the free medical clinics are.

_____ 6. I can live without a car.

Could you survive in middle class?

(Put a check beside the items you have experienced or know how to do.)

_____ 1. I know how to order in a nice restaurant.

_____ 2. I talk to my children about going to college.

_____ 3. I understand the difference between the principal, interest, and escrow statements on my house payment.

_____ 4. I know how to help my children with their homework and do not hesitate to call the school if I need additional information.

_____ 5. I understand my term life insurance, disability insurance, 20/80 medical insurance policy as well as the need for house insurance, flood insurance, and replacement insurance.

_____ 6. I know how to get a library card.

Could you survive in wealth?

(Put a check beside the items you have experienced or know how to do.)

_____ 1. I have several favorite restaurants in different countries of the world.

_____ 2. I know how to read a corporate financial statement and analyze my own financial statements.

_____ 3. I have at least two residences which are staffed and maintained.

_____ 4. I know how to enroll my children in the preferred private schools.

_____ 5. I am on the boards of at least two charities.

_____ 6. I fly my own plane, the company plane, or the Concorde.

Figure 3–1. *Hidden Rules Among Classes: A Quiz—excerpted from* Poverty: A Framework for Understanding and Working with Students and Adults from Poverty, *(Payne 1995, 83–89).*

access to a kind of "success" as measured by dominant culture standards. However, the underlying assumptions about power, control, and exclusion are never directly addressed.

According to Payne, educators can neither excuse nor scold students for not knowing these hidden rules. Instead, any supportive adult should, in her words, "teach them and provide support, insistence and expectations" (8). While it is important to be aware of the conflicting class-based codes or assumptions when confronting difference, it takes more than good intentions by liberal educators for students to succeed.

Power and White Middle-Class Liberal Assumptions About School. Lisa Delpit (1995) takes Payne's assessment one step further in her analysis of the imbalance of power and the dynamics of inequality in America's schools. In her book *Other People's Children: Cultural Conflict in the Classroom,* she critiques several statements typical of those made with the best of intentions by White middle-class liberal educators. "To the surprise of the speakers," she asserts, "it is not unusual for such content to be met with vocal opposition or strong silence by people of color" (28). While her critique is certainly informed by the politics of racial domination, Delpit argues that it is also the dominant assumptions of the middle class that shape these remarks and lead to cultural dissonance in the classroom. Below I examine three of these statements Delpit quotes that seem particularly relevant to assumptions guiding the field of drama and theatre in education along with relevant examples from my own experience:

1. "I want the same thing for everyone else's children as I want for mine." (28)

I recently went to an awards ceremony honoring academic excellence at my eighth-grade stepdaughter's middle school. Morgan was receiving an award. Entirely too many parents were squeezed into the hot gymnasium. Fans whirled to keep the crowd as comfortable as they could but with little effect. The event itself was mind-numbing as name after name was called—first the sixth graders, then the seventh graders, and finally eighth graders. Slowly it dawned on me that there had only been one or perhaps two Latina/o students receiving awards out of over 300 students being recognized. I know Latina/o enrollment at the school is much higher than that. This school draws heavily from an affluent community that has folded itself around a lake, with lakeside homes valued from $200,000 to a million dollars; others students come from a poor and working-class community across the highway, where most live in mobile homes and must drink bottled water due to poor water services.

When I asked Morgan why there were so few Latina/os receiving awards, she shrugged and said, "They keep to themselves. Those kids really gang together." I asked what she meant. After fits and starts she finally explained, "They don't show good leadership skills—so they don't get awards." The simple desire for equality does not guarantee equality. Given her class affiliation, Morgan has had access to more usable "cultural capital" than many students of color. She has been provided with ample experience in how middle-class culture operates—its formal language structure, its rewarding of leadership, its attention to achievement and personal best. To ensure that students with less of this kind of cultural knowledge are not penalized, Delpit advises that schools need to provide students with the discourse patterns, interactional styles, and spoken and written language codes that will allow them success in the larger society. At home, she points out, parents are transmitting another culture in order to survive in their communities. What are we as drama and theatre educators and practitioners doing to aid this process?

Through improvisational drama, for example, I recently conducted a court case with a group of Latina/o fifth- and sixth-grade students who created a fictional situation concerning three students who had been accused of possessing drugs on school property. After some background improvisations to establish the situation, the class brainstormed and divided up the roles we would need to enact a court trial. Individually and in groups the prosecutors, defendants, and witnesses had to organize themselves, prepare their arguments or statements, prepare evidence, present statements, use formal language registers, follow court procedure, and make summary statements to the press during our week-long trial. In between drama sessions, the students discussed the connection between what they were doing and televised court cases they had seen and other situations where the use of formal language is important. We also discussed key political concepts such as "justice for all" and puzzled over how accurately it reflected our experience. By self-consciously understanding the importance of calling attention to these kinds of codes with young people who ordinarily don't have access to them *as well as* reflecting on and critically discussing the social systems we currently have in place, drama educators and theatre practitioners are well positioned to help effect change through their practice.

2. "Child-centered, whole language, and process approaches are needed in order to allow a democratic state of free, autonomous, empowered adults, and because research has shown that children learn best through these methods." (31)

It's a hot afternoon in May. School will be out next week and the kids are excited. We are outside because the small portable where we usually have class is just too hot and too confining for the raw energy of the group. I've been doing drama twice a week with this class of fourth graders on a variety of curricular topics during their 1994–95 academic year. We've done games about habitat and survival, created improvisations that led into persuasive and descriptive writing, role-played problems facing communities, and even made video ads promoting healthy choices. Since things are winding down, the students have asked if we can just play games today.

We are currently in the middle of the second level of a dramatic version of "Red Light, Green Light." The students imagine that they are trying to escape from jail and the person who is "It" is their guard. With her back to everyone, the guard can turn and look *anytime* she wants at the large group of prisoners who are busy trying to sneak up behind her to steal her keys. Whenever she turns, everyone must instantly freeze. If she sees *anyone* moving, the *entire group* has to go back and start over. It requires team work and cooperative effort to get the "keys" and get out of "jail." But since we had been working together in similar kinds of ways for some time, I was fairly confident that they would be able to do this without too much trouble. However, it's not going well. The group has been sent back four times now. And the students are hot and sweaty and getting restless.

Suddenly Kroshawnda explodes, "I hate this stupid game. I ain't playing no more."

"It *is* hard. But how can we try to solve the problem?" I try to redirect and not sound patronizing, as sweat trickles down my back. "What can we as a group do?"

"I don't care. I ain't playing no more. Tha's it." She storms off. I'm really surprised. Kroshawnda has been volatile with her classmates in the past, but never to me. I, of course, pursue her. I've worked for a year to gain her trust and encourage her to believe in herself. I'm not letting her give up now.

"Kroshawnda. Listen to me. Quitting doesn't solve anything." She ignores me. I finally grab her shoulder to try to stop her.

"Get offa me!" she says as she jerks away.

"What's your problem? I can't believe you're acting this way! Why can't you just work with everybody and get this figured out? It is not that hard!" I realize I'm screaming. Kroshawnda glares at me, her hostility is palpable. I know what she's thinking: Who does this pathetic White woman think she is—my friend or something?

"Jus' leave me alone," she pleads. She turns and stomps off across the playground. Sweat is pouring down my face; it is sweat, isn't it? Where the hell is the teacher? I suddenly notice that all the other kids are staring me as if they can't believe what just happened. I look at my watch; we still have twenty minutes left and their regular teacher is nowhere in sight.

"Well," I sigh and take a deep breath, "I guess we learned that it's hard to solve problems when we can't get along." It sounds weak and the group knows it. Some students are eyeing me suspiciously for the first time this whole year. Suddenly I'm just like all the rest of the teachers. I ask what they want to play next and we continue with a simple game of tag. They don't really need me. Why do I need to *think* they do?

Two questions emerge from this incident. First, how does a drama teacher deal with the conflicting skills of cooperation *and* individual achievement—especially in a middle-class competitive world? I often found that students in less affluent schools didn't know "what I wanted" when we would embark on cooperative work—a phenomenon I found less often with students in more affluent schools. I also found that instructions for open-ended work were often too vague for students to grasp, making me appear somehow flaky and uncertain. Delpit advises that teachers shouldn't deny students access to themselves as a source of knowledge necessary for them to learn what it is they need to succeed (32).

Which brings up a second question: How do you wield power as a drama and theatre educator in ways that make cultural and pedagogic sense? Interestingly, White middle-class teachers often resist exhibiting power in the classroom. I know I have. "Somehow to exhibit one's personal power as expert source is viewed," as Delpit observes, "as 'disempowering' one's students" (32). How can we help students solve problems—that is, share our outside eyes, expertise, and give solid direction—within firm boundaries so students can work with confidence in the comfort of fixed perimeters? How can we develop the confidence to "limit to free," as the late Barbara Salisbury Wills counseled?

3. "It's really a shame but she (that Black teacher upstairs) seems to be so authoritarian, so focused on skills and so teacher directed. Those poor kids never seem to be allowed to really express their creativity." (33)

After school I am sitting in an empty classroom waiting for the teacher to return so we can discuss why things haven't been working out as I thought they would. "Everybody thinks it's easy for me to teach these kids 'cause I'm Black. Well, you know what?" the teacher says as she walks back in, shaking her head. "It's not easy for me to teach these kind of kids. It's not easy at all."

In the spring of 1996, I asked a veteran African American teacher I'll call Barbara if I could work in her fifth-grade classroom. I was interested in her teaching style—and her authoritarian and strict reputation. Unlike other teachers I have worked with, who have been fairly enthusiastic about drama work, Barbara sat at her desk whenever I taught a drama lesson. Not unlike other students I had worked with in this school, however, her class had an extremely hard time working in groups. And an even harder time accepting each other's ideas. After school one day I asked Barbara to help me understand what was going on with the students.

"You wanta know why they act the way they do? They don't have *nothing*. And they probably won't *ever* have nothing, either. I at least give them discipline. They know what's what and they can count on it."

In Barbara's room I noticed a real difference in how power and authority were displayed. She was very direct, explicit, and concrete. She had earned her role as teacher through her authority. I tried to sort out what she was doing differently. First, Delpit notes that middle-class and working-class speech patterns tend to differ (34). Middle-class directives are often stated as a question (more like a veiled command); working-class directives are more overt. Secondly, a tendency with drama teachers is to adopt a "one-of-the-gang stance"—which for most working class or working poor signals one who has no authority (35). Many liberal middle-class teachers tend to want to downplay their authority—through softspoken attempts to reduce the implication of overt power in order to establish a more egalitarian and nonauthoritarian classroom atmosphere. But if children operate under another notion of authority—you run into trouble, Delpit warns. Those children will more likely than not be labeled as behavior problems and sent to special education or suspension.

For example, in Barbara's class I often had trouble redirecting certain students into the work. One student in particular was a very angry young man prone to violence. Although Carlos had volunteered a few times to take on roles in our improvisational work, he confined himself to strong male power positions such as a father, a principal, and a police officer. I could tell by her rapt attention whenever Carlos would play a role that his involvement concerned Barbara.

One day, I made the mistake of putting my hand on Carlos's shoulder to acknowledge that he was talking out of turn and needed to pay attention. He bolted up—glaring at me hatefully. I had definitely crossed a line. Without any discussion, Barbara sent him to the principal's office. That semester several students were asked not to participate in our work by Barbara and instead were sent out for Content Mastery or to the library—a first for me in all my years of drama teaching. Although I know Barbara was trying to impose limits and possibly protect me, at what point does conflict over student behavior become a clash between differing student and teacher cultural knowledge and expectations? How do we make sure we analyze this as a teacher's problem and not a child's?

Economic Advantage—The Other Story. Most of the attention in this chapter has been on examining the impact of social class standing on poor or working-class students. Students from economically advantaged class positions have their own sets of issues which can be equally as disorienting for educators or theatre workers from less advantaged backgrounds. For example, the first time I taught in the College for Kids program for high-achieving elementary students at University of Wisconsin, I was amazed at the high verbal level of the group of fifth-grade students I found myself working with for an intensive week. Not only was this group of all White students from economically privileged backgrounds, they had all been involved in Talented and Gifted programs at their respective schools for several years. Fascinatingly, they refused to participate in some of the opening cooperative and improvisational activities I had planned for the first day. We ended up doing very little drama and a great deal of talking. I was baffled.

That evening I spent a few hours in the library researching "talented and gifted" issues. I soon realized that these students were probably so accustomed to positive reinforcement for achievement, and rewards for their "talents" and "gifts" that they were terrified to try something at which they might fail—in front of strangers, no less. Instead, they used their superior verbal skills to scoff at the exercises, representing the work as beneath them and consequently something that couldn't possibly hold their interest. "Aren't we going to do a play?" one asked on the first day as I tried to cajole them into an improvisation. A play was at least a familiar, fixed entity in which they could perform and shine individually for their delighted parents, which would reinforce the students' need for approval of their "gifts." No, we would not be doing a play.

After the first day I changed tactics and hooked them intellectually into a mystery situation for which they could use their verbal and logic skills as investigators (a role not too distant from their own individual subject positions and desires). Eventually the situation demanded that we "simulate" certain moments together to find more clues. It worked and, despite the torturous beginning, the students were reluctant to end our drama on the last day of class.

Johnny Saldaña (1999b) at Arizona State University noted a similar problem when he conducted a Forum Theatre workshop with two high school student groups from contrasting social class positions: one from a less economically advantaged area and one from a much more advantaged environment. The students were charged with creating scenarios concerning oppression that would then be improvised and reworked according to the group's ideas about how else the protagonist might deal with the situation of oppression.

The reactions to the workshops were very different. The less advantaged group fully engaged in the workshop and identified several scenarios to do with what Saldaña calls the problem of "horizontal hostility," that is, a peer group versus a stigmatized individual. For these adolescent students, the individual fear of being labeled as "different" and therefore excluded from various peer groups is something that resonates with their nondominant social group membership and affects their personal struggle with their emerging identities.

Conversely, Saldaña notes that the students in the more economically advantaged group did not choose to explore adolescent themes. Instead, they enacted "material reminiscent of television sketch comedy and theatre sports" (9). Their scenes, which included such topical subject matter as the President coercing a Secret Service agent to cover up his sexual indiscretion, had more to do with showcasing their "perceived comedic talents" rather than seriously examining oppression or contemporary social issues (10). In the end, the group chose to explore a scene in which a homeowner is trying to get rid of an aggressive door-to-door vacuum cleaner salesperson to exploit its comedic potential. Saldaña noted that in the "interventions" that followed, these privileged students subverted his authority as the facilitator of the experience in favor of their own desire to "perform," denied the existence of social issues in their world, blatantly stereotyped the working-class salesperson, and ignored others' ideas in favor of their own (10). Saldaña elaborates:

> Like a targeted adolescent, I became a victim of group ridicule. This socially self-conscious, upper-class group excluded me from their cultures of adoles-centrism and privilege. They denied my agenda for social issues exploration by transforming theatre from an art form that examines the human condition, into shallow entertaining diversion. My pedagogical desires were negated; like the broad brushstroke we apply to those with wealth and power, their needs came first. (11)

As a side note, Saldaña mentions that one of his student teachers also tried to do Forum Theatre work with a group of affluent high school students who also rejected the issue-oriented topics as just "too *Afterschool Special*" for them (11).

While it is important for educators to introduce middle-class codes to those who don't have access to them, this example illustrates that those in more dominant positions need to be exposed to skills that encourage critical thinking about the world around them and their relative position in it. Power succeeds, as Terry Eagleton (1990) asserts, through its persuasiveness—making collusion desirable (37). If theatre makers and educators are interested in examining and interrupting the dominant class-based power dynamics that allow or inhibit equal access to educational opportunity, then we need to conduct our work in ways that accommodate and challenge students who occupy a range of social positions.

Building Awareness

The following lesson plans provide a framework through which to address important issues associated with social class:

TOPIC: SOCIAL CLASS—SOCIAL POSITIONS

Focus What kinds of social positions make up a kingdom?[2]

Teaching Objectives

To discuss various social class positions in an imaginary kingdom and the preconceptions people in those different positions might have about one another;

To explore the issues and challenges that those preconceptions may cause for different members of social class groupings;

To reflect on how we might change those preconceptions.

Target Age K–3rd grade

Time Needed Two 45-minute sessions

Materials

- Photograph or picture of a castle.
- *King Bidgood's in the Bathtub* by Audrey Wood with illustrations by Don Wood (San Diego: Harcourt Brace, 1985). To the dismay of his court, a jolly king refuses to get out of the bathtub and rule his kingdom.

Procedure

1. ENGAGE the students: Show a photograph or picture of a castle. Ask several questions about what the photograph is, where it might be located, who might live there, etc. Mention how big it is: *Who might work there? What kinds of jobs do people do in a castle?* Ask individual students (and possibly the whole group) to pantomime their suggestions. *Let's look at a story in which something peculiar happens at a castle that causes a great deal of work for someone who works there.*

2. SHARE the story: Gather students. Tell the students the title of the story, *King Bidgood's in the Bathtub,* and spend a few minutes looking at the front cover. Engage them in predicting what might happen: *Who might these people be? What seems to be going on? What can you tell about how they might be feeling? What might they be thinking? Let's see what happens.* Read the story up to the section where the entire court is in the bathtub with the King for the masquerade ball. Pause to discuss the various illustrations as you read. Ask about the various jobs people are responsible for—particularly the Page. *Different people have different jobs. What is the King responsible for? What do the members of court seem to be responsible for? What about the Page? What is the Page doing now?*
3. EXPLORE the story:
   a. Count and freeze pantomime: Ask students to imagine they are one of the members of the court. They have just heard that the King wants to have the masquerade ball in the bathtub! They need to get ready for the ball, bathtub or not. What do they do? Have students find a space in the room and on a three-count ask them to create a frozen statue of how a member of the court might stand. Starting from this frozen position, slowly count to five to give students a controlled opportunity to explore how they might get ready for the ball. (This can also be done with appropriate music—begin the exploration when the music starts. Freeze when the music stops.) Sidecoach as needed: *What might you decide to wear? How would you put it on? How does it feel to move with your costume on?* On five, ask students to freeze. Comment on what you see. (For example, *I see some interesting things people are doing with their bodies that make me wonder what kinds of costumes these members of the court are wearing. I see some terrific facial expressions that make me wonder what these members of the court are feeling.*) Ask the students to relax and for volunteers to show what they were doing. Encourage the observers to ask questions.

      Repeat the entire exercise from the point of view of the Page. Sidecoach as needed: *I wonder how the Page might be feeling at this point? What can you do with your body and your face to show those feelings? I wonder how the Page might prepare for this big event? What things might the Page be asked to do? What equipment or supplies might the Page need?* Share. Ask students how each experience was different from the other. *What did each character do or think about that was different?*

b. Frozen image: With half the class create an image of King Bidgood in the tub surrounded by the various court members and the Page. Ask for a student to volunteer being the King and take a position and freeze. One at a time ask the other students in the group to join in. Ask the last student to place themselves as if they were the Page. When the image is set, ask the observing students about the various characters: *How might the members of the court be feeling? What is it about what they are doing with their bodies and their faces that tells you that? What might they be thinking? What might they be about to say?* Ask the same questions about the King and the Page. With the other half of the class, use the same process to create an image of the entire court in the bathtub with the last person in the group placing themselves as if they are the Page. Muse: *The place is a mess! I wonder what the Page is going to do now.*

c. Discuss: Gather the group to discuss the Page's dilemma: *How will the Page manage all the work? What can the Page do?* Depending on their suggestions and your comfort level with drama, try enacting the student's different solutions using improvisation in either small groups or as a large group. For a more focused drama experience, wonder aloud what would happen if the Page could get more help. Proceed as follows:

d. Teacher in role: As the Page, address the group. "*Thank you all for coming so quickly. I didn't realize so many people would be needing jobs at the moment. But I can sure tell you that I need the extra help. Here's the problem: the King is in the bathtub and he won't get out! He's having his meetings in there, his meals in there, and even a masquerade ball—which is getting ready to start any minute. There are so many things to do. I need help organizing all the chores. I've never been in charge of anything quite like this before! I know many of you have worked for the King in the past so you know something about this. What do you think we need to do to prepare for the evening's event?*" Solicit many suggestions and write them on the board or on a flip chart. Prompt with questions as needed about how to handle food, water, mopping up, dirty dishes, wet clothing, towels, and so on. Ask volunteers to take responsibility for the various jobs that need to be done. Everyone should have a job.

e. Scene work: Try one or more of the following:

   1) a scene in which all the workers gather their supplies and report for duty;

2) a scene in which half the group are in the bathtub and half the group are workers ready to take care of business. The Page may want to introduce the new workers to the court and then play out an initial scene with interactions between the court and the workers. (Planning what might happen in the scene before it starts can help younger students stay focused.)

3) a "fast forward" scene in which there is no dialogue, just double-time action. (Planning key events is crucial in a scene like this.)

4) a scene in which the workers meet and talk about all the work they have been doing and how tired they are. Teacher in role as the Page, who complains: *We have to find a way to get the King out of the tub. I'm so tired I can't keep this up! What can we do? Let's put our heads together and see if we can solve this problem.*

5) various scenes or frozen images that show how the workers try to get the King out of the bathtub. Ask: *How well do you think this solution worked? What is it about this idea would make the King come out of the tub?*

6) read and enact the end of the story to see how the Page solved the problem in the book.

4. REFLECT on the issues: Engage students in a discussion that explores the attitudes of the various people in the story to one another: *How did the King treat the courtiers? Why? How did the courtiers treat the King? Why? How did the courtiers treat the Page and the other workers? Why? How did the Page and the other workers treat the courtiers? Why? Whose jobs seemed most important? Why? If you were to rank the jobs which would be first and which would be last?* (This can be done on the board or with volunteers assuming the roles of various people who do various jobs and having the class line them up. Name tags with the name of the character or job can help keep characters straight.) *Does everyone agree with this ranking? How might you rearrange them?*

   Engage in a discussion about what the people in this story might get paid for the work they do: *Let's think about how much these different people might get paid for their jobs. Who do you think makes the most money; who makes the least amount of money? Why?* Rank their answers and compare the relative importance of the job with the pay received. Ask the students if they think this is fair. Many young children identify with the Page and think that job should receive the same money as the court. Ask the students to imagine that they are in charge of how money is distributed in this kingdom. *How would you determine how much people are paid for the type of work that they do? Some people may not agree with your ideas. What reasons could you give them for your opinions?*

5. EVALUATE the lesson: What did you notice about the group's willingness to discuss this issue? Was there any reluctance to engage? If so, why? What stereotypes were brought up? How do you feel you handled them? How did the students portray people from different class positions? What things still need to be examined? What questions did you have trouble answering? Which discussion segments worked best? Why? What do students seem most interested in concerning this issue? Based on your evaluation, how might you follow up this lesson?

Possible Extensions

Language Arts

Write a letter to King Bidgood about one of the following: how he should organize his kingdom and salaries, a recommendation for a reward for the Page and the workers in recognition of their hard work and cleverness, an application for a job at the castle.

Social Studies

List all the jobs needed to make things work in your community. How would you rank them in importance? Find out how much people get paid for these jobs. Compare and contrast your rankings with actual salaries. What would you change?

Math

Consider various math problems around hourly wages, annual salaries, and the cost of necessary goods such as food, housing, transportation.

Drama

What happens to a kingdom if the Page and all the workers go on strike?

TOPIC: SOCIAL CLASS—THE IMPACT OF POVERTY

Focus How do a boy and his father survive on little income?

Teaching Objectives

To discuss various preconceptions about poverty and its impact on people, focusing on homelessness;

Figure–3-2. Fly Away Home *by Eve Bunting.*

To explore the issues and challenges facing those who are homeless, including other people's attitudes and assumptions about them;

To reflect on how we might change preconceptions about the homeless.

Target Age 4th–6th grade

Time Needed Two 45-minute sessions

Materials

- A key on a long ribbon or string.
- *Fly Away Home* by Eve Bunting with illustrations by Ronald Himler (New York: Clarion, 1991). A homeless boy named Andrew and his father survive difficult circumstances by living in an airport, moving from terminal to terminal trying not to attract attention to themselves.
- Map of a major airport detailing the main terminals (available in any airline magazine and many travel books).

Procedure

1. ENGAGE the students: Hold up the key and ask students to consider what it might be for. Categorize their suggestions (place to live, transportation, place to keep things safe, etc.). Ask everyone to imagine that

it is a key to a place someone calls home—a house, a trailer home, or an apartment. Discuss: *We all have different images of what "home" means to us. What does "home" mean to you? What kinds of things come to mind when you hear the word "home"? Having a place to live or shelter is a basic need of all living creatures, including people. But not everyone has a key that lets them into a place to live. People who find themselves homeless for various reasons try to find other ways to take care of the basic need for shelter. Let's look at a story about a how a boy and his father manage by living in an airport.*

2. SHARE the story: Either read or tell the story *Fly Away Home.* Key questions to explore include: *What does it mean to "not be noticed?" Why would someone not want to call attention to themselves? How do you avoid being noticed? How do you know who to trust? How do people find themselves in situations like this?*
3. EXPLORE the story:
    a. Pantomime improvisation: In small groups, ask students to create a pantomimed scene of people either leaving or arriving at an airport. They should pay close attention to characterization, relationships, and detail. After ample work time, share the scenes with the whole. (If students have limited experience with drama this can be done improvisationally as a large group with six volunteers or half of the group at a time. Structure the activity as an add-on improvisation with one person starting with an action or attitude and others joining in to flesh out relationships, tensions, and so on.) Ask the rest of the class to carefully observe what is going on. *Who are these people? What is their relationship to one another? Are they coming or going? What tells you that?*

       After one or two scenes have been shared, ask a group to freeze at the end of their improvisation and ask observers to add in a person or two who might be facing the same situation as Andrew and his father. Ask how the new character(s) will avoid being noticed. Run the scene for one minute and see what happens. Discuss: *How easy was it to not be noticed? How easy was it to not notice? What kinds of attitudes do people with homes and extra money have about people who don't have those necessities? Andrew seemed to have some pretty strong feelings about people with money. What kinds of attitudes do you think people who are homeless might have about people who aren't? I wonder how Andrew and his father got into this situation.*
    b. Photograph Album: Create a series of images of Andrew's past life. Either brainstorm possible pictures that might be in a photo album of Andrew's life or hand out cards with titles like On the day

Andrew was born; Happy Birthday, Andrew!; Our favorite pastime; The funeral; Goodbye, Park Street; Under the stars; etc. Discuss the order the photos should be viewed in and speculate on what information each photograph tells us about Andrew and his economic circumstances.

c. Discuss: *We've learned quite a lot about Andrew and his father. I wonder how they would respond to other people knowing about their story. What do you suppose might happen if a news team wanted to do a cover story on people who live at the airport? What about the need to avoid "being noticed"? What if they get caught because of the exposure by the news team? Would a TV story help or hurt their situation?*

d. Teacher in role: Address the group as the producer of a documentary news show, *That's the Way it Is: "Glad you all made it to this early morning meeting. We have a lead on a really exciting story that one of the reporters brought to my attention last night. When he came in on a late flight, he started talking to one of the baggage handlers while he was trying to track down his lost luggage. It turns out there is a small population of homeless people that live at the airport. Apparently they try to disguise themselves as travelers and drift from terminal to terminal. Who else has heard about this phenomenon? What kinds of things have you heard? How do they avoid getting caught by security? If we want to do a cover story on this issue, what do we need to know?* (Record responses on a chalkboard, a flip chart, or overhead. Ask the group to categorize areas of information needed, such as sleeping arrangements, personal care, school, avoiding security, etc.)

Here's a map that shows the major terminals at the airport. How should we proceed to organize ourselves in order to cover the story as thoroughly as possible? Anything we need to watch out for? (Record suggestions and any concerns the group brings up.)

e. Scene work: Try one or more of the following:

1) In small groups, compose "video" clips of a reporter trying to interview a homeless person. The interview is interrupted for some reason. What happens? Who ends the interview? For what reason?

2) Andrew and his father are noticed by security as a result of the reporters. In small groups, create a scene that explores what happens as they try to "pass" as travelers.

3) As a large group plan how the news program about the homeless situation at the airport should be represented and reported. Who else

should be interviewed? (Airport personnel, the mayor, other travelers, security, civil rights lawyers, etc.) Divide up the work and create a written and/or performed version of the news program. (The performed version could be videotaped for further analysis.) What point of view does the program take on the issue? Why?

4. REFLECT on the issues: *What are the pressures on people as they try to survive difficult economic pressures? What attitudes do some people have about people who find themselves without basic necessities? How does the media help or hinder an understanding of issues like homelessness? If you could give advice to the editor of that program, what would you say?*
5. EVALUATE the lesson: What did you notice about the group's willingness to discuss this issue? Was there any reluctance to engage? If so, why? What stereotypes were brought up? How do you feel you handled them? How did the students portray people from different class positions? What things still need to be examined? What questions did you have trouble answering? Which discussion segments worked best? Why? What do students seem most interested in concerning this issue? Based on your evaluation, how might you follow up this lesson?

Possible Extensions

Language Arts

Create letters to the editor that someone might write about the issues brought up in the news report.

Examine the kinds of attitudes that people might have about the homeless. Write a poem that reflects how homeless people might feel about those attitudes.

Social Studies

What kinds of community structures support groups of citizens? How did supportive structures develop in the homeless groups at the airport? How did people look out for one another? Research how that happens in other groups of homeless people. What services are currently available for the homeless? How effective are they?

Drama

What might a group of homeless people removed from the airport have to say to their city council about affordable housing?

Creating an Environment for Equity

While I recognize that generalizations do not apply to every case, I have observed certain behavior patterns in relation to class status in my work with young people and from my own social class experience. To summarize, my experience has been that students from poor or working-class environments often:

- have limited parental involvement in their school or family life;
- have limited access to staple items such as food and stable housing;
- have limited access to material possessions such as computers, books, educational supplies, clothes, travel;
- often have self-esteem issues; have lower expectations of themselves and others;
- are used to getting by;
- are better with short-term planning than long-term;
- are organizationally challenged;
- distrust those who don't use their hands in some way to make a living;
- have a general distrust of power figures (whether teachers or police);
- are accustomed to sharing whatever they do have; and
- have a keen awareness of their underclass status.

Students from situations of economic privilege often:

- have a high degree of parental involvement in school and family life;
- have parents with some higher-education background;
- have ample access to basic needs such as food and housing;
- have ample access to material goods (educational supplies, books, travel, etc.);
- have strong verbal and reading abilities;
- are not aware of their class status as important;
- are fairly well organized;
- engage in long-term planning including thinking about college;
- know how to achieve on tests and please teachers;
- involved in extracurricular experiences; and
- are competitive.

What do we as drama practitioners do with this information? First and foremost, be sensitive to context—your own and others. Carefully examine your own social class background and your enculturation into the codes with which you are familiar and assume are "normal" knowledge. Actively seek out information about social class positions that are not your own. Second, look for opportunities to discuss and expose the ways in which class domination operates in your work. For example, in a drama about search and seizure with a group of fifth and sixth graders from a working-poor neighborhood, I stopped the drama after a "teacher" character announced he was going to search everyone's backpacks to look for a stolen item. This gave us the opportunity to discuss how decisions about rights are made when age is a factor and how similar or different the situation might be given the social class or racial makeup of the presumed offenders.

Third, infuse your work in ways that teach the class-based codes and skills that are needed to participate fully in American life, regardless of where your students or audiences lie on the social class spectrum. Rather than viewing the teaching of these codes as an assimilationist tactic, I prefer to believe that these codes cannot be meaningfully contested unless they are openly examined and understood.

The expected outcomes could be viewed as a kind of "empowerment." However, this word often has paternalistic connotations and is somewhat vague in its humanistic idealism of human betterment. Today, I prefer to couch possible outcomes as "educating for access and awareness"—which is sorely needed if we are ever going to reach the point at which those operating and transforming the social institutions in our country match the diversity represented in our population. As Trinh T. Minh-ha (1986–7) suggests, however, "there are no social positions exempt from becoming oppressive to others—any group—any position can move into the oppressor role" (6). For those of us who work in education drama and theatre, the key is to be watchful and reflexive about our pedagogy and our practice.

Questions to Ponder

1. How would you describe your own relationship to class? When were you aware of it? What made you aware of it?
2. Describe how class is "inscribed" in the streets of your community.
3. How do you see the values of the middle class in operation at your school or working environment? What can you do to make sure all the young people you come into contact with succeed?
4. Should affirmative action shift its emphasis away from race and ethnicity to economic disadvantage? Why or why not?
5. How can teachers effectively engage in conversations about privilege and power with affluent students?

Practical Problems to Consider

1. Working with a retelling of *Snow White,* how would you make sure that a variety of social class positions are equally and fairly represented?
2. Knowing that organization can be an issue for many people in situations of poverty, what steps would you take to ensure that students were sufficiently ready to present a ten-minute play at a school assembly?
3. When working with an economically advantaged group of youth, several students make comments about how stupid construction workers and secretaries are. How do you respond?
4. You are working with a group of students of mixed social class backgrounds. Students tend to lump themselves into self-selected economic groupings. How might you acknowledge this segregation and encourage dialogue between these two groups through drama practice?
5. A kindergarten colleague wants to use drama in her unit on occupations and has asked you to help her plan. How might you create an activity that would value occupations across the social class spectrum?

A Case Study Situation

You have been asked to conduct an afterschool enrichment drama program at a school with a 90 percent free lunch program. Two students in your group are homeless. When you ask the group what topics they are interested in doing drama about, they decide on home, occupations, and money. How do you embark on the drama work in ways that respect the material circumstances of your students yet provide a critique of "normalized" myths?

Resources for Drama and Theatre Work on Social Class

Books for Young People

A Day's Work by Eve Bunting (New York: Clarion Books, 1994). A Mexican American boy tries to help his grandfather find work and learns an important lesson.

The Cook and the King by Maria Cristina Brusca and Tona Wilson (New York: Henry Holt, 1993). A cook gives wise counsel to a stubborn and bossy king.

The Garden of Adbul Gasazi by Chris Van Allsburg (New York: Houghton Mifflin, 1979). A dog runs away and ends up in the opulent garden of a contentious magician. Nice illustration of different social class environments.

Pool Party by Gary Soto (New York: Delacourt Press, 1993). A working-class ten-year-old is invited to a pool party by the richest girl in town. Everyone tries to give him advice on how to behave.

Radio Man by Arthur Dorros (New York: HarperCollins, 1993). A family of migrant farmworkers rely on the radio to help connect them to family and friends in the different places they live.

Plays

Just Before Sleep by James Still (available from Dramatic Publishing at 203-254-6624 or e-mail: <dramaticpb@aol.com>.) A moving story of a mother and her two children who struggle to survive homelessness.

Journey of the Sparrows by Meryl Friedman adapted from the book by Fran Leeper Buss (available from Dramatic Publishing at 203-254-6624 or e-mail: <dramaticpb@aol.com>.) Four young refugees from El Savador are smuggled to Chicago where they attempt to earn a living and avoid deportation.

Five Good Resources for Drama and Theatre Work on Social Class Issues

Linkon, S. L. 1999. *Teaching Working Class.* Amherst, MA: University of Massachusetts Press. An excellent collection of innovative approaches to class-conscious pedagogy.

Payne, R. 1995. *Poverty: A Framework for Understanding and Working with Students and Adults from Poverty.* Baytown, TX: RFT Publishers. A former public school principal gives a straightforward analysis of the culture of poverty and the hidden class codes that govern most educational institutions.

Ryan, J. and C. Sackry. 1984. *Strangers in Paradise: Academics from the Working-class.* Boston: South End Press. A moving collection of stories by working-class educators who recount how they cope with being "caught between two worlds."

Rodriguez, R. 1982. *The Hunger of Memory.* New York: Bantam. An account of a working-class Latino student's process of cultural separation as he progressed through educational institutions.

Smith, L. "Some General Values of Working Class Culture." A useful chart outlining basic attitudes and experiences that affect working-class students. On the Web at <http://members.aol.com/lsmithdog/

bottomdog/WCValuespost.htm>. The chart can also be found in Smith's article "Working Class Matters: Myths and Values," *The Heartlands Today* 6 (1996): 35–44.

Notes

1. See Kozol (1991) for a more complete discussion of the complex inequities in school funding.

2. This lesson is adapted from an idea shared by Trish Prentice in my creative drama class at the University of Texas in the fall of 1994.

4

Gender Reorientations

constructing "girls" and "boys"

"If we want to understand gender inequality, it is much more important to shift from an analysis of difference per se *to an analysis of the ways in which the social structure privileges some people's differences at the expense of others'."*

—SANDRA LIPSITZ BEM, IN *RACE, CLASS, GENDER IN THE UNITED STATES.*

"Okay. Can I get y'all to come over here? I need y'all to come over here please." A nervous preservice teacher is gathering a coed group of sixth-graders to begin a dramatic activity. She explains that in just a moment they will be transported to a beach scene where a murderer is on the loose. This murderer can only "kill" by winking and when he or she winks at you, you are supposed to "die" very dramatically. The murderer will try to keep their identity a secret but if anyone has a guess, they are allowed to stop the drama and make an accusation. If they are wrong—well, of course, they die. All in all, a pleasant activity that young people seem to love.

"I need y'all to shut your eyes now so I can pick a murderer." After she silently picks a student to play the murderer, the leader asks everyone to open their eyes and wonders how many of them have ever been to the beach. Several students raise their hands. "If we were to create a beach scene in here," she asks, "what would you be doing?" However, before the students have a real chance to answer, she quickly adds: "The girls would probably be sunbathing and the boys would probably be playing volleyball or something, right? Okay, why don't you imagine that this big empty space is a beach and take your positions. When I say 'go,' the murderer will be on the loose."

I swiftly grab my notebook to make a note and when I look up again, I notice that all of the girls are lying on the floor. "Are they dead?" I wonder. I had not heard any dramatic deaths yet—but that doesn't always mean anything. I then realize that, no, they are just girls who have been assigned to yet another inactive role in a drama. They are "sunbathing" while the boys are running around all over the "beach" overly excited about the murderer who is now on the loose and just winking at boys.

Interestingly, when I bring up the problem during our evaluation session I find that no one had noticed it. They were completely focused on how to control the boys and paid little or no attention to what the girls were doing—or not doing. How often does this happen in a girl's experience of school? Critics such as Myra Sadker and David Sadker (1994) report that despite the gains in gender equity over the past thirty-five years, the messages girls *still* receive in school is that they are "worth less" (13). "Like a thief in the school," Sadkar and Sadkar submit, "sexist lessons subvert education, twisting it into a system that robs potential." The costs of sexism can be enormous—loss of academic achievement and sense of self for girls; the reinforcement of limiting social identities and empathetic responses for boys. How do teachers inadvertently contribute to gender role stereotyping in their drama work? How do limiting assumptions about gender roles affect identity formation? How can drama teachers and theatre for youth practitioners actively avoid these traps as they structure dramatic situations?

ABC's of Gender

Analyzing gender as an identity location requires a close look at how we understand the differences between girls and boys biologically as well as at the social and cultural expectations of gendered roles. Parents, caregivers, and teachers all play an important part in how girls learn to be girls (women) and how boys learn to be boys (men). In this chapter, I analyze the relationship between gender and biology, the construction of gender by various social systems, the difference between gender roles and gender identity, the ways in which gender is learned and rewarded in our culture, the way language helps shape and reinforce our understandings of gender, and ways in which drama practice and pedagogy can interrupt limiting gender role stereotypes.

The lesson plans included in this chapter illustrate how a classroom teacher or drama practitioner can encourage young people to carefully examine these issues through drama as a way to build awareness and empathy and to set the tone for ongoing discussions. Younger elementary students give advice to a young woman who is trying to start her own "dragon control" business. Older elementary students are introduced to Ruby, a young girl who tries to thwart her parents' expectations about her future by engaging in several "reckless" activities. Both groups are asked to analyze stereotypical gender expectations and consider how they might redefine what it means to be a girl or boy.

The last part of the chapter lists several hands-on suggestions for teachers and practitioners to help create a climate for gender equity and awareness in classroom interactions and theatre work. The resources listed should prove to be useful starting points for interrupting gender stereotyping in and through our work.

Analyzing Gender

In "How Society and Schools Shortchange Girls and Boys," Duane Campbell and Dolores Delgado Campbell (1996) point out strong similarities between sexism and racism:

> Both are oppressions. Both teach role relationships that leave one group in a subordinate position. Both are primarily expressed through institutional arrangements of privilege for some and oppression for others. Both are forms of violence: individual and collective, psychological and physical. (109)

As with racism, issues pertaining to equity, access, and the protection of the basic civil rights of those whose are adversely affected by sexism become pressing social concerns. And as with racist attitudes, gender role expectations and sexist assumptions are learned as young people grow and develop. In this light, it becomes doubly important to more fully understand how gender operates as an identity location in the development of young people.

Not unlike race, "gender" as a concept can be usefully understood as a socially constructed and highly political identity category. Feminist theorist Ruth Hubbard (1998) points out that the social categories of "girls" and "boys" are socially determined roles into which young people try their best to fit (32). How successfully young people adapt or conform to these predetermined categories has particular social consequences. Consider the following incident: I was recently walking into an ice cream shop just as an agitated mother was hurriedly ushering her daughter out by the arm. Once on the sidewalk, the mother stopped and began to lecture: "You don't burp in public." "Why?" the girl asked innocently, if not sheepishly. "Because it's bad manners. Very bad manners." "Oh," the girl said, taking in the comment. "And besides," the mother quickly added, "it's just not ladylike." At this the

Figure 4–1. *"Welcome . . . to the land of the free, where even a 150-foot-tall green French woman can get a job!"* "Liberty" actress: Krista Shafer in "Liberty!" by Chris Wells from COOTIE SHOTS: *Theatrical Inoculations Against Bigotry,* created and produced by Fringe Benefits Theatre. Los Angeles premiere, October 1999. COOTIE SHOTS: *Theatrical Inoculations Against Bigotry* published by Theatre Communications Group, fall 2000. Costume designer: Martha Ferrara. Photo by Kathi Kent.

girl looked genuinely perplexed. As Hubbard argues, what it means to be a "girl" (and to grow into a "lady" as this instance illustrated) is reinforced through various admonishments for transgressions as well as rewards for doing the "right" thing. As Simone de Beauvoir so clearly articulated in 1953, "One isn't born a woman, one becomes a woman" (249).

What Is the Difference Between Biology and Gender? An immediate assumption is that there is a one-to-one correlation between biology and gender and that somehow biology determines the role men and women should play or are able to play in society. For example, as inconceivable as it seems now, there once was a time when women were perceived to have smaller brains than men, which was interpreted as meaning that they were not meant to study and that studying would distract blood that should be flowing into their reproductive organs by diverting it to their brains (Hubbard 1998, 33). While this reasoning seems completely absurd now, physical differences (such as a tendency towards muscularity in men or monthly menstruation in women) are still thought to somehow define what is possible or appropriate activity within a narrow definition of male and female gender roles.

In their excellent "Sexism Curriculum Design" in *Teaching for Diversity and Social Justice,* Diane Goodman and Steven Schapiro (1997) define biological sex as "the physiological and anatomical characteristics of maleness and femaleness with which a person is born" (115). Biologically speaking, there is little difference between males and females beyond reproductive functioning and distribution of muscles. While some cognitive differences have been scrutinized in previous research on math, verbal, and spatial skills, Sadker, Sadker, and Klein (1991) report that the disparity in these differences has been declining, according to a recent study that attributes these improvements to changes in socialization, child-rearing, and schooling (309). What was once thought to be biologically predetermined is now seen to be socially constructed and passed on.

Gollnick and Chin (1998) point out that anthropologists have noted a great deal of variation in perceived gender differences from culture to culture (122). Anthropologist Henrietta Moore (1990) states that "the images, attributes, activities, and appropriate behavior associated with women [and men] are always culturally and historically specific" as opposed to biologically predetermined (7). As literary theorist Myra Jehlen (1995) summarizes, "culture, society, history, define gender, not nature" (263).

A Distinction: Gender Roles and Gender Identity. Gender, therefore, refers to the set of assumptions about abilities and expectations that are socially constructed. Further, we each struggle to negotiate between our biology and the predetermined gender expectations that surround us in the struggle to locate our individual gender identities. Feminist theorist Judith Butler (1990a) warns, however, that "gender ought not to be construed as a stable identity . . . rather, gender is an identity tenuously constituted in time" (140). Identity formation is a fluid process, not fixed, and constantly shifting as we discover new information that amends our previous understandings.

Goodman and Schapiro (1997) make the following distinctions between "gender role" and "gender identity":

> *Gender Role* refers to the socially constructed and culturally specific behavior and expectations for women (femininity) and men (masculinity).
>
> *Gender Identity* refers to one's psychological sense of oneself as a male or female. (115)

A problem arises, as in the case of racism, when the experience of one identity location is privileged over another. In this case, male experience is privileged over female experience in American culture despite a political system that purports to be democratic and therefore gender-neutral. However, as feminist psychologist Sandra Lipsitz Bem (1998) points out, there is in play a disguised set of standards or norms that are organized in favor of and around male experience (49–50). As a result male/female difference is reduced to female weakness or disadvantage when measured against a male set of "norms." In addition to the assumptions associated with narrowly defined gender role expectations, women are measured in terms of what they "lack" in order to be competitive with men outside their "normal" sphere. This information gets passed on to young people in many different ways. For example, a teacher who needs help carrying things from one room to another might pass over girls who volunteer to help in favor of boys whose arms are perceived to be stronger and, by extension, not "weak" like a girl's.

Awareness of the workings of sexism and the continual struggle for access to social power is crucial to creating more equitable classrooms and interactions with young people. Goodman and Schapiro provide useful definitions of sexism and social power:

> *Sexism:* The cultural, institutional, and individual set of beliefs and practices that privilege men, subordinate women, and denigrate values and practices associated with women.
>
> *Social Power:* Access to resources that enhance one's chances of getting what one needs in order to lead a comfortable, productive, and safe life. (117)

As recent reports put out by the American Association of University Women (AAUW) have revealed, equity in schools still has a long way to go.[1] For example, in *Gender Gaps: Where Schools Still Fail Our Children,* the AAUW states that the prevailing classroom climate is still one in which teachers describe girls' strengths as "good behavior, the desire to please the teacher, and general attention to assigned tasks" which the researchers point out can actually work against them because teachers are often preoccupied by boys' "poor behavior" (1999, 62). This was certainly the case in the story at the start of this chapter. Whether sexism takes the form of grossly blatant harassment or unwitting covert comments about what is considered "ladylike," access to resources and opportunities has been denied.

Various articulations of feminism have played an important part in rethinking gender. Feminist theatre critic Gayle Austin (1990) clearly articulates that "a feminist approach to anything means paying attention to women" (1). Toril Moi (1986) points out that feminism is necessarily a political position

(204). Certainly, in order to increase social power (as defined above), a feminist lens focuses on how girls learn about prescribed gender roles *and* how boys are granted and enculturated into privilege can be useful to drama educators and theatre practitioners.

Constructing Girls

As we listen to lectures like the one that firmly placed burping on the list of "unladylike" activities, we are from birth imprinted with gendered assumptions. From the early associations of the color pink, to adults cooing over "preciousness," to frilly dresses and bows, girls soon learn what will bring praise and what will not. Similarly, along with the initial associations of the color blue, boys hear murmurs of "slugger," "big guy," "little man," and act accordingly. Judith Butler (1990b) points out that "performing one's gender wrong initiates a set of punishments" (279). Performing it correctly provides a comforting reassurance that all is well.

Besides learning about gender expectations from parents, caregivers, and other adults, Mary Pipher (1994) in her widely read book *Reviving Ophelia* notes the impact of the media on girls. She asserts that today's girls are more oppressed than ever as they attempt to come of age in what she terms "a more dangerous, sexualized and media-saturated culture" (12). Girls are bombarded with messages from a variety of media sources, what Clarence Page refers to as the "electronic wallpaper" of our lives, about how they should look, dress, and act, as well as what they should consume (quoted in Pipher, 27). Sexualized images of dangerously thin young women are used to sell everything from soft drinks to cars. Pipher notes a "girl-poisoning" tendency in contemporary music, television, films, and advertising (12). The impact of the media along with the shift in agency from preadolescence into adolescence often results in dramatic behavior changes. "Girls become 'female impersonators,'" Pipher notes, as they stop considering their own desires and concern themselves with what others may want them to be.

Journalist Peggy Orenstein was inspired by the AAUW's 1991 report, *Shortchanging Girls, Shortchanging America,* to investigate more thoroughly what girls were learning about gender identity and agency through an intimate portrait of girls she interviewed in two different school contexts. In her book *Schoolgirls: Young Women, Self-Esteem, and the Confidence Gap,* she notes a discrepancy in how girls see themselves and what they do. In her words:

> Without a strong sense of self, girls will enter adulthood at a deficit: they will be less able to fulfill their potential, less willing to take on challenges, less

> willing to defy tradition in their career choices, which means sacrificing economic equity . . . They will be less prepared to weather the storms of adult life, more likely to become depressed, hopeless, and self-destructive. (1994, xxviii)

While our present social system privileges male experience, it does so at a high cost to girls and women. Girls learn early on to replicate gender inequality as they construct gender identities around deference to men.[2] For example, as I have been working on this book, the U.S. women's soccer team won the World Cup. The effect has been a staggering victory for women's sports and the controversies just as interesting. Besides bringing into the open the issue of equal pay for female athletes, the decision by several team members to pose for swimsuit ads or, as in Brandi Chastain's case, nude in sports ads has raised some compelling questions. Are these young women merely finding ways to increase their earning potential to be more on par with male athletes or are they objectifying themselves and colluding with a sexist preoccupation with the female body as a commodity? Or are they victims of the advertising industry, who while compensating them well for their images will make enormous profits from their likenesses? Despite the soccer victory, have the subsequent endorsements reinforced the notion that girls and women are more valuable socially as objects to be looked at—what Pipher calls "lookism" (98)—rather than as active agents in their own right?

Constructing Boys

When I first entered this field, I worked as a storyteller traveling from school to school conducting week-long residencies in K–6 classrooms throughout the Midwest. I searched diligently for stories that had female protagonists. This was in the early 1980s and I found inspiration in stories such as Robert Munsch's *The Paper Bag Princess*, the "Three Strong Women from Japan," and "Tatterhood." And when I couldn't find stories with strong female protagonists, I would adapt or simply make them up. For example, the "Five Chinese Brothers" (a problematic story because of ethnic stereotyping) became the "Five Silly Siblings" with non-gender-specific names like Fishbait, Bobber, Sinker, and Fly Catcher. "Ask Mr. Bear" became "Ask Ms. Bear"—you get the idea. It was important to me for reasons I could not quite articulate at the time. I just knew I wanted the girls in the classes I visited to feel enfranchised and represented as strong-willed and confident. In retrospect, I wonder if I obliterated the representation of boys, or worse, reduced them to stereotyped bumblers or ne'er-do-wells like all the Jacks in the Jack tales. I noticed early on in my own upbringing that the dissonance produced by gender differences

Figure 4–2. *An argument over allowing girls into the boys' clubhouse in* I Remember Ernie *by Matt Buchanan (Produced by the University of Texas at Austin).*

between boys and girls was enormously unsatisfying. The world I inhabited privileged one gendered experience over another—a situation that I would struggle with throughout my life.

While the emphasis of much of the concern about gender dynamics in the classroom has to do with girls, I do not want to overlook the pressures boys feel as they, too, struggle with their understanding of gender expectations and identity. William Pollack (1998), in his best-selling *Real Boys: Rescuing Our Sons from the Myth of Boyhood,* asserts that boys are just as confused as girls are about the mixed messages they receive and are in effect forced into a "gender straightjacket" by what he calls "the Boy Code" (6). The Boy Code, Pollack explains, encourages young men to be stoic, to exhibit bravado, to achieve status and dominance, and to restrain from showing feelings (23–4). In a rather superficial way, Pollack insists that the Boy Code can be unlearned and that boys can be find their inner sensitivity. While this is one of the few volumes that focuses on boys and what they think about gender role expectations, Pollack's work would benefit from a more focused analysis of the politics of gender and, in particular, how gender is portrayed in present-day culture. *Real Boys* is not unlike Mary Pipher's work, in that young people's voices and experiences are essentialized at the expense of a broader critique of gender dynamics. The fact remains that sexism benefits men and boys on some levels; it also exacts a toll on their ability to break out of rigidly defined gender norms.

Developing a Sensitivity to Gender Bias. In their helpful article titled "Gender and Educational Equality," Myra Sadker, David Sadker, and Lynette Long (1997) outline six forms of gender bias used to evaluate teaching resources (132–34). These include linguistic bias, stereotyping, invisibility, imbalance, unreality, and fragmentation. While originally intended to aid in the evaluation of curricular materials, I have adapted these criteria to provide a useful way for us to evaluate subject matter and form in drama and theatre work for young people.

1. **Linguistic Bias:** This is the easiest form of bias to identify and includes the exclusive use of masculine terms and pronouns as well as references to women as wives or male possessions. For example, referring to characters in source material only by their relationship to a man (such as the Seal Wife) rather by name, reinforces sexist assumptions and erases the possibilities for independent female identity construction. Supposedly innocent popular phrases are also guilty in this regard. For example, in the U.S., we have assumed that the term "you guys" is inclusive of everyone when, in reality, it is not. Language matters.
2. **Stereotyping:** Stereotyping in drama and theatre work for youth occurs not only in the representation of female characters but also in how boys and men are portrayed. By continually picking source material or enabling improvisational work that depicts boys as adventurous, brave, and athletic and girls as dependent, fearful, and passive, drama teachers and practitioners contribute to negative constructions of gender. A variety of career choices can be enacted to break out of restrictive understandings of possible futures.
3. **Invisibility:** Sadker, Sadker, and Long cite a curriculum survey that found males pictured twice as often as females in textbooks and in three times as many occupations (133). This absence is felt across the curriculum and often in drama and theatre work. Drama teachers and theatre practitioners should evaluate their lesson plans, seasons, and outreach offerings to make sure they are not playing a major role in this disappearing act.

4. **Imbalance:** By only privileging one version of an issue or event, many textbooks and curriculum sources perpetuate bias. This is certainly the case in the study of history. In drama and theatre work, we have the opportunity to play with stories and source material from multiple points of view and to actively consider the investments of each point of view. Joe Winston (1998), for example, offers an excellent treatment of "Jack and Beanstalk" which features several perspectives on the antics of Jack and the Giant. Through discussion and complex dramatic structuring, students begin to grapple with the fact that both characters are morally flawed.[3]
5. **Unreality:** Often curriculum materials feature nuclear family scenarios quite prominently when, in reality, about 50 percent of marriages end in divorce. As families continue to be reformed and reconfigured, Sadker, Sadker, and Long remind us of our obligation to create a variety of familial groupings in our work with young people (133).
6. **Fragmentation:** Much of what is included about women in the curriculum focuses on sporadic unique contributions rather than on a sustained understanding of women as integrated into the larger social fabric and work force. We should be wary of just doing a "gender" drama or a "famous woman" play as a way to address positive attention to women. Constant and vigilant attention to how males and females are represented in our work will result in fewer gender-biased outcomes.

To actively engage in the practice of a pedagogy that seeks to provide greater access and equity for all students, teachers or practitioners can evaluate their practical work using these criteria. More than anything, teachers need to continually educate themselves about gender equity issues and recognize when bias is at work—if even if it has occurred unintentionally. The more aware we are, the better our chances of creating environments through which young people can build their own awareness of gender and identity.

Building Awareness

The following lesson plans represent two age-appropriate explorations of the subject of gender. Younger elementary students are introducted to the issue through a role drama extension of the picture book *The Paper Bag Princess,* while upper elementary students puzzle out the possible negative effects of limiting gender expectations on boys and girls.

Figure 4–3. *A drama leader encourages frank and open discussion about stereotyping and prejudice.*

TOPIC: GENDER ROLES— CHALLENGING STEREOTYPES

Focus How can a young woman succeed despite limiting stereotypes?

Teaching Objectives:

To discuss gender-based stereotypes and preconceptions about boys and girls;

To explore the issues and challenges that those stereotypes may cause for girls and boys;

To reflect on how we can work to change those stereotypes.

Target Age K–3rd grade

Time Needed Two or more 45-minute sessions

Materials

- A bone. (Real or fake. The bigger the better.)
- *The Paper Bag Princess* by Robert Munsch with illustrations by Michael Martchenko (Toronto: Annick Press Ltd., 1980). A young woman out-

wits a dragon in order to save her fiancé, only to realize that his views about women are disappointing.

Procedure

1. ENGAGE the students: Gather the students in a circle. Place the bone in the middle of the circle. Ask them to consider what it is, what it came from, why it might be here. *Bones are things that are left behind. How do you suppose this one got left behind?* (Listen to student predictions.) *Well, this bone reminds me of something pretty astonishing that happened to a young woman named Elizabeth when she got herself involved in tracking down a dragon. Lucky for her, this dragon left a trail—of bones just like this one. Let's see what happened to Elizabeth.*
2. SHARE the story: Read or tell the story of *The Paper Bag Princess.* Take time to ponder over how truly horrible this dragon is and try to calculate just how much he has eaten in one day. *If you were Elizabeth, how would you start looking for this dragon?*
3. EXPLORE the story:
   a. Narrative pantomime: Ask the students to spread out around the room. As they listen to your narration, they should move and respond to everything you say as if they were Elizabeth. Start by having everyone sit down and hold their heads in their hands.

      Well, it started out to be a nice morning. But it's been one of those days. You let out a long, loud sigh. Where should you begin? You stand up and dust yourself off. You scratch your head. Start by looking down, you think. Hey, what's that over there? You walk over a few steps, bend down, and see the definite shape of a dragon's footprint. You hold out your hand and are able to trace out the shape with your pointer finger. Yep. That's him, all right. You start to follow the prints. Suddenly, you stop and stand stone still. You don't move a muscle. The only thing that moves is your eyelashes when you need to blink. Yuck. What IS that?! Something is lying on the ground in front of you. Something big. You bend down and slowly pick it up. It's white and hard and smelly. As you hold it up you realize that it's a bone. Great. Probably from a horse. You throw it down and wipe off your hands. You realize you are dealing with a very dramatic dragon. You take three giant steps. One. Two. Three. You put your hand up to keep the sun out of your eyes. You think you see something glinting in the sun. Gotcha! There's a giant door over in the distance. You eagerly run up to it. The door knocker is pretty tall. You have to reach up on your tiptoes. But you grab it and knock as hard as you can. The door slowly creaks open. And there, in all his glory, is a big green smelly dragon.

b. Dragon machine: Gather the group and comment on their movement and expressiveness as they played Elizabeth. The next task is to create the dragon. Ask for one volunteer to come to the center of the space and place themselves in an appropriate position (either with or without movement and sound) and then have others add on one at a time until the group is happy with their creation. Let individuals step out to look at it and make suggestions. Ask the dragon to walk, to roar, and to breathe fire.

c. Scene work: Using the strategies the group came up with to portray the dragon, play out the scene in which Elizabeth outwits him. Ask the group to plan where to begin and what needs to be said. End the scene just as the dragon falls asleep. After playing it through, ask the group to evaluate their scene. Is there anything they could do to make the story clearer? Replay if students have suggestions.

d. Teacher in role: Set up an initial discussion about Elizabeth's further adventures. *We know that Elizabeth went on to live a happy life, but what exactly did she do?* Ask the students to brainstorm. (Build on one of their ideas or proceed with the following situation.) *Well, one of the many things she did was start a School for Dragon Defeaters. When it first got started she had a little trouble finding clients. She finally had to ask for some help advertising her school. Would you mind becoming those people for a moment? When I sit down, I'll become fearless Elizabeth.* Make a clear distinction about when you are in role and when you are not. Do not be afraid to stop the drama if you need to clarify what is going on.

Oh my! I didn't realize they were going to send the whole advertising team! Well, I'm glad you are here because I have a huge problem. I have this great school with these great classes to teach these great things about dealing with dragons . . . but most people still don't think that a girl knows anything about this kind of stuff. I've tried to let people know that I'm here, but I've only had one person come—a boy—and when he found out that I taught all the classes he just said, "What do girls know about this kind of stuff?" and left. This is my dream. And I'm not going to give it up. But I need some help. What can I do to get more people interested in my school? Let the students ask questions and make suggestions. Possible questions might include: What classes does the school offer? How long is the course? Is there any kind of certificate? Is there any kind of internship or hands-on experience with real dragons? Press the students to think about ways to change the opinion that girls don't know anything about bravery or self-defense. Out of role, encourage the students to make a list of their ideas and suggestions and to identify the various tasks they need to do in order to create a good advertising campaign for Elizabeth's school.

e. Scene/project work: Depending on their ideas, have students do one or more of the following:
   1. Create a print ad campaign.
   2. Create a television commercial or infomercial.
   3. Create a billboard on butcher paper.
   4. Create a radio ad using an audio cassette player.
   5. Create a brochure.
   6. Create business cards.

   Continue to challenge the students to question stereotypical ideas about what girls can or cannot do. Share scenes or projects and discuss.

4. REFLECT on the issues: *What kinds of stereotypes did Elizabeth bump up against? How did the members of the advertising agency try to address those stereotypes in their advertising work? How successful were they? What will it take for people to stop making stereotypical assumptions about what girls and boys are supposed to be like?*
5. EVALUATE the lesson: What did you notice about the group's willingness to discuss this issue? Was there any reluctance to engage? If so, why? What stereotypes were brought up? How do you feel you handled them? How did the students respond to the discussion of gender roles? What things still need to be examined? What questions did you have trouble answering? What discussion segments worked best? Why? What do students seem most interested in concerning this issue? Based on your evaluation, how might you follow up this lesson?

Possible Extensions

Language Arts

Create a "textbook" or course handout for one of the classes at Elizabeth's school.

Health

Explore further information about gender role expectations. What information about gender do young people learn from the media? Ask students to keep a log for a week and discuss their observations.

Science

Look at the bone structure of several different creatures. Where did the bone we used in our drama come from?

Are dragons real? Research the history and mythology of dragons.

TOPIC: GENDER ROLES—THE EFFECTS OF GENDER ROLE EXPECTATIONS

Focus How does being a boy or girl affect how you act and what you do?

Teaching Objectives

To discuss gender-based expectations, stereotypes, and preconceptions about boys and girls;

To explore the issues and challenges that those stereotypes may cause for girls and boys;

To reflect on how we can work to change those stereotypes.

Target Age 4th–6th grade

Time needed Two 45-minute sessions

Materials

- "Vote with Your Feet" statements about gender role expectations (see below); the phrases "I agree," "I disagree," "I'm not sure" written in large print on three different pieces of paper; tape.
- *Reckless Ruby* by Hiawyn Oram with illustrations by Tony Ross (London: Picture Lions, 1992). To counteract her parents' ideas about her future as the "precious" wife of a prince, Ruby sets out to act as reckless as she can to avoid this fate.

Procedure

1. ENGAGE the students: Explain that today's topic has to do with the expectations and assumptions we think our culture has about what girls and women should do or be like and what boys or men should do or be like. To help assess student knowledge, received understandings, and current opinions, clear a space in the room and tape three signs on the wall or floor in the following order: I agree, I'm not sure, I disagree. Read the following statements one at a time and ask students to "vote with their feet" and stand by the sign that best expresses their opinion. Without making judgments, ask one or two representatives from each of the major clusters of opinions why they made that choice.

For example, if the statement "I think girls should watch their weight," results with many girls clustered around "I disagree" while many boys cluster around "I agree," ask one or two people from each cluster to talk about why they agree or disagree with the statement. Muse about how it is that girls learn to think about the issue/statement/question in one way and how boys learn to think about it differently. (It can sometimes be useful to keep track of these musings on the board for later reference.) If useful, try the statement with the opposite gender subject (e.g., "I think boys should watch their weight") and compare results. Possible statements include:

I think girls should be soft-spoken.

I think boys should carry things when needed.

I think girls should be afraid of bugs.

I think boys should never cry.

I think women should stay home and men should work.

I think women should be the ones who take care of children.

Because I am a boy or girl, I might baby-sit.

Because I am a boy or girl, I might wear jewelry.

Because I am a boy or girl, I could be a doctor.

Because I am a boy or girl, I might play with dolls.

Because I am a boy or girl, I might kiss my mother.

Because I am a boy or girl, I might play basketball.

Because I am a boy or girl, I might dress like the other gender in a play.[4]

Discussion: *This exercise brought up many different opinions about the roles we are expected to play in our families, community, and society. What is a role?* (Roles can be defined as ways of thinking, being, or doing things; a set of behaviors that have been labeled.) *These labeled ways of behaving often have certain expectations associated with them. If someone has been labeled a "bully," what expectations would you have? If someone has been labeled the "class clown" (or "teacher's pet," etc.) what expectations would you have? Gender roles are the expectations people have about how girls and women or boys and men should behave. This affects personal relationships, family relationships, and the possibilities for your future. As you saw, there are different opinions about what those expectations are or should be. Not all expectations or the assumptions that go along with them are true or fair. Even so, those expectations often affect your behavior and the way you think you have to act. What can you do to change that? Let's look at a situation in which a girl tried to change the expectations her parents had about her future because she was a girl.*

2. SHARE the story: Read or tell the story of *Reckless Ruby*. Periodically discuss why she chose to do some of the things she did. *What stereotypes or gender expectations was she trying to challenge? How successful was she?*
3. EXPLORE the story:
   a. Image work: In small groups, ask the students to create a frozen image of one of Ruby's reckless adventures. Share images. Facilitate the observation and discussion by asking, *What do you see going on here? What can you say about body language? Facial expressions? What can you say about the relationships between the various people in this picture? What tells you that? What might they each be thinking? Feeling? What might they be getting ready to say? What gender expectations or stereotypes is Ruby trying to challenge here? How successful was she?*
   b. Discussion: *I wonder how you get people to change or at least modify their expectations about you or about other people. Let's set up a situation in which some specialists might have become concerned about Ruby's well-being. Who might those people be?*

      Let students decide on the type of specialists, how they found out about Ruby, why they are concerned or alarmed, and where they might meet to discuss this. (Possibilities include one or a combination of the following: police officers, child protection services, school counselors, psychiatrists, doctors, researchers, authors, investigative reporters, and so on. These individuals may have found out about Ruby through medical reports, anonymous tips, news reports, referrals, rumor, or other sources.) Depending on student input, set up or modify the following teacher-in-role section.
   c. Teacher in role: Ask the group to arrange the space for a meeting of the specialists. After the space is set up, ask the students to quietly consider who they might be in this scene. *What kind of expertise do you have? Where do you work? How did you find out about Ruby? Why are you concerned about her? What name or title will you use to introduce yourself to the others?* Ask them to help create the world of this story by silently walking in one at a time and freezing in a position they think says something about their character and the particular kind of expertise they have. They can be sitting or standing. After all students are place, call the meeting to order from the vantage point of a mediator role with a "second in command" status.

Welcome the group. Tell them you appreciate their time and concern. *We all want to help this young woman and by the end of the meeting we will hopefully have some concrete ideas about what we can do.* Since they do not know one another well, have them introduce themselves and their area of expertise to the rest of the group. Tell the group that you want to get right to the point and get their concerns on the table. Stress how destructive gender role expectations can be and how to change people's views and educate parents and others. Ask the group to brainstorm possible action plans. Record their ideas. Group and classify ideas as needed to help clarify their thoughts. Encourage the group to make a plan they feel they can execute. Ask for volunteers to implement various aspects of their plan.

Out of role, discuss the meeting, the issues and ideas that were raised, and the action plan. Speculate: *How effective do they think the plan will be? How might some people respond? and so on.*

d. Scene work /art work /computer work: In groups, tackle the action plan. Examples of possible action include: developing educational materials; meeting with Ruby's parents; showing a video of one of Ruby's actions to her parents or other concerned groups; putting Ruby and her parents on a talk show; setting up a meeting between Ruby, a counselor, and her parents; sending her parents to a gender awareness camp; creating a "girls rule" campaign on the Internet. Share scenes or work with the other groups. Ask observers to think critically about the work.

4. REFLECT on the issues: *What are the negative effects of gender role stereotyping? Why do people have these kinds of expectations? Who benefits? Who might be harmed? What can we do to change this?*

5. EVALUATE the lesson: What did you notice about the group's willingness to discuss this issue? Was there any reluctance to engage? If so, why? What stereotypes were brought up? How do you feel you handled them? What things still need to be examined? What questions did you have trouble answering? What discussion segments worked best? Why? What do students seem most interested in concerning this issue? Based on your evaluation, how might you follow up this lesson?

Possible Extensions

Language arts

Write a news story about Ruby and her exploits.

Social studies

Examine the achievements and biographies of several strong women and adventurous women such as Sally Ride, Amelia Earhart, Dian Fossey, Florence Griffith Joyner, etc.

Drama

Create a play about Ruby's experience and journey. Share it with other classes or grade levels.

Health

Connect this lesson with discussions about other kinds of role expectations, self-esteem issues, and goal setting.

Creating an Environment for Equity

As teachers and drama practitioners striving to create learning environments with an eye toward greater equity, how can our practical everyday pedagogy reflect an awareness of gender and gender bias? According to Gollnick and Chin (1994), healthy, nonsexist classroom environments include settings in which gender is not the determining factor in how students are sorted, grouped; that do not grant boys a preferred status over girls; that depict both genders in a variety of emotional, action-oriented roles as well as free exploration of traditional and nontraditional roles; and finally, that provide space for students to develop positive attitudes about sexuality (141). Following Sadker and Sadker (1986), below are some hands-on things drama teachers and theatre directors can do to help create an ongoing awareness of gender equity in work with young people:

- Confront gender bias rather than ignore it.
- Work to interrupt segregation and reinforce coed work.
- Train young people in peer leadership and cooperative group skills.
- Use a range of literary materials as a base for your work, with a balance between strong female and male protagonists and a range of family situations and support networks.
- Remember that language matters.
- Be aware of equity in your questioning strategies.
- Avoid reinforcing limiting stereotypes in process work.
- Avoid limiting representations of gender and sexuality in performative work.

- Have students track and evaluate their work in light of equity issues.
- Continually educate yourself about equity issues.

Questions to Ponder

1. How would you describe your own relationship to gender expectations? When were you first aware of gender differences? What made you aware of gender expectations?
2. How are gender expectations affecting the students you ordinarily interact with?
3. How would you describe gender relations at your school or in your working environment? What are the benefits? What are the costs?
4. Does affirmative action help alleviate or reinforce gender bias? Why or why not?
5. Some people believe that the way to eliminate gender-biased education is to move to single-sex schools. What are the pros and cons of single-sex schooling? Can you create a "gender-relaxed" atmosphere in a coeducational setting?

Practical Problems to Consider

1. Working with a retelling of *Cinderella* as a source for creative drama or theatre work, how would you structure the event so that stereotypical understandings of gender are examined?
2. Knowing that boys often take over leadership roles in small-group activities, what steps would you take to ensure that students working to develop an original play were sufficiently prepared to work together equitably?
3. While working with a single-sex group of girls, you notice several comments are made about how dumb and insensitive boys are. How do you respond?
4. You are working with a coeducational group of students who are resisting paired work with the opposite sex. How might you acknowledge their discomfort and encourage discussion about the issue through drama work?
5. A fourth-grade colleague wants to use creative drama in a Health unit on sex role stereotypes and has asked for your advice. What activity

might you suggest that includes an understanding of how male and female gender roles are constructed by society?

A Case Study Situation

Your school or theatre group has received a grant to create a theatre piece about the media's influence in shaping gender roles and gender expectations with a coeducational group of fifteen interested fifth-grade students. Consider how you would begin exploring the issues and how you might move toward shaping this work.

During the process, several students insist that scenes depicting stereotypical male and female roles should be included because "they are funny." You want to avoid "rehearsing" stereotypes in your performance, but how do you respond?

Resources for Drama and Theatre Work on Gender and Sexism

Picture Books

Abuela by Arthur Dorros (New York: Dutton Children's Books, 1991). A girl wonders what it would be like if she and her grandmother could be picked up by birds and fly all over the city of New York.

Gina by Bernard Waber (Boston, MA: Houghton Mifflin, 1995). Gina moves to a new building and discovers she's the only girl there.

I Look Like a Girl by Sheila Hamanaka (New York: Morrow Junior Books, 1999). A young girl becomes anything she wants (including a jaguar, a condor, and a dolphin) in her imagination.

My Outrageous Friend, Charlie by Martha Alexander (New York: Dial Books for Young Readers, 1989). A girl who admires her outrageous best friend realizes she can be outrageous, too.

Tough Boris by Mem Fox (New York: Harcourt Brace, 1992). A greedy, scary pirate cries when his parrot dies.

Plays

Selkie by Laurie Brooks Gollobin (in C. Jennings' *Theatre for Young Audiences: 20 Great Plays for Children,* New York: St. Martin's Press, 1998). The daughter of a selkie, a grey seal, struggles with her physical difference in this coming-of-age story.

Tomato Plant Girl by Wes Middleton (forthcoming from Dramatic Publishing at 203-254-6624 or e-mail: <dramaticpb@aol.com>). A unique visitor causes tensions between two friends in this play for young children.

Five Good Resources on Gender and Sexism Discussed in This Chapter

Gender Gaps: Where Schools Still Fail Our Children. 1999. Commissioned by the American Association of University Women Educational Foundation. New York: Marlowe and Company.

How Schools Shortchange Girls: The AAUW Report, A Study of Major Findings on Girls and Education. 1992. Researched by the Wellesley College Center for Research on Women. Washington, D.C.: American Association of University Women Educational Foundation.

Orenstein, P. 1994. *Schoolgirls: Young Women, Self-Esteem, and the Confidence Gap.* New York: Doubleday.

Pollack, W. 1998. *Real Boys: Rescuing Our Sons from the Myth of Boyhood.* New York: Henry Holt and Company.

Sadker, M. and D. Sadker. 1994. *Failing at Fairness: How Our Schools Cheat Girls.* New York: Simon and Schuster.

Notes

1. See *How Schools Shortchange Girls: The AAUW Report, A Study of Major Findings on Girls and Education* (1992), *Hostile Hallways: The AAUW Survey on Sexual Harassment in America's Schools* (1993), *Gender Gaps: Where Schools Still Fail Our Children* (1999).

2. See Bem (1998) for a more complete discussion of this point.

3. For a full description of this drama structure, see Joe Winston (1998), 123–143.

4. This exercise incorporates curricular information a fifth-grade teacher shared with me about sex roles and sex role stereotyping. Unfortunately, this material was on a handout and was not credited to any source. Regardless, I have found these statements to be a useful way to open up discussion about gender issues with young people.

5

Sexual Orientations

same-sex feelings and families

"Educators significantly influence the experiences of . . . boys and girls in school. It is the educator who chooses how *to teach the prescribed sexuality curriculum; it is the educator who challenges or winks at homophobic comments or jokes among students; it is the educator who comforts or ignores a student suffering from the heterosexist tirades of peers or doubts about her sexual identity . . ."*

—JAMES T. SEARS, *COMING OUT OF THE CLASSROOM CLOSET*

"I have a question for you about Emily's moms," the fifth-grade teacher begins. "Are they married," he asks pointedly. "Are her two moms a married couple?" The class thoughtfully ponders the question about a family situation depicted in a prize-winning Mother's Day essay written by a girl in their school about her lesbian moms.

"If they want to get married they can," one student ventures. "Or they can just live together—like my old day-care teacher. She lives with a man and they're not married but it doesn't really matter."

After some initial discussion, the teacher gives the students a little more background. "Today the law says that if you are the same sex—two men and two women—you can't get married," he tells them. "It is against the law." As the students take this in, the teacher asks them to pretend for a moment that they are a group of judges trying to make a decision about this issue. "Some people think that it's wrong for gays to get married, that it's not natural, and that it goes against what a family is," he explains. "Other people think that the state should not decide these things—that it

Figure 5–1. *Including gay people in a social studies lesson on stereotypes. From* It's Elementary: Talking About Gay Issues in School.

should just be up to two adults to decide what they want to do. What do you think?"

In small groups, students heatedly debate the issue. "I don't see why they shouldn't," one young woman offers. "But one might have a disease," a young man interrupts. He is insistent on making a connection between same-sex marriage and disease and presses the point, although he never mentions AIDS directly. "But," another young woman counters, "a man and a woman could have a disease also like that."

In another group, one young woman announces, "I think that gay people should get married. If you love someone, let them be married." She points to two boys in her group and asks them to imagine they are in love. "If I am the judge," she hypothesizes, "and I say, 'No, you two can't get married. I don't care if you love them. You can't get married,' how do you think you guys would feel?" "Mad!" says one of the boys. "Yeah, exactly!" she declares, having proved her point.

In another group a student has turned the tables: "What if the majority was gay or lesbian couples and there was a law that said you *had* to be gay or lesbian and you couldn't get married to the opposite sex? I think they [heterosexists] should think about that and see how they would feel and then they might know how gays and lesbians feel." However, a boy in the group is quite frustrated by this logic. "But they want other people to be gay! They think they want to be the bosses of other people." Others in the group immediately take issue with his comment as their discussion continues.

This lively exchange is from *It's Elementary,* a 1997 documentary focusing on how various teachers have addressed gay and lesbian issues with elementary and middle school students in age-appropriate ways. Produced by Women's Educational Media, its goal is to increase respect for a more inclusive understanding of diversity in American culture. However, adding a consideration of gay civil rights to a multicultural education agenda is often fraught with controversy. Rich classroom discussions, like the one discussed above, are rare.[1] The pervasiveness of heterosexism has resulted in the near absence of any substantive discussions about the denial of basic civil rights to gays and lesbians in schools. The issue of marriage is only one of many civil arenas in which gays and lesbians have no power. At this writing there are no federal laws to protect gays and lesbians from discrimination in the workplace despite the fact that laws protect individual rights relative to race, gender, religion, national origin, and disability.[2]

Far from being discussed on a par with racism and sexism, heterosexist assumptions prevail in our classrooms as well as at the national level. In schools, homophobic behavior is tacitly condoned as teachers ignore name-calling and jokes that degrade gays and lesbians. "It's amazing how teachers don't notice what's going on," one student comments in *It's Elementary.* "It makes you feel weird in your stomach." In many areas, teachers or theatre makers who want to address these issues with young people fear reprisals from powerful conservative factions. The cost of this silence is enormous. Young people struggling to understand their sexual identity feel bereft if they do not fit the norm. Each year over 30 percent of teen suicides are gay or lesbian related (Harbeck 1992a, 3). In addition, hate crimes aimed at gay and lesbian people are escalating at an alarming rate and have in fact tripled since 1991 ("Hate Crimes" 1999). If, as is estimated, 10 percent of the population is gay or lesbian, how can teachers and drama practitioners sensitively respond and uphold the rights of *every* student?

ABC's of Sexual Orientation

Analyzing sexual orientation as an identity location requires a closer look at the normative assumptions about sexuality that are pervasive in American culture. Negative attitudes about same-sex relationships need to be contrasted

Figure 5–2. *"I don't think people should be strict about [gay people], because if they were gay, they wouldn't want to be getting beat up . . ."—4th grader. From* It's Elementary: Talking About Gay Issues in School.

with the impact of those attitudes. If the cluster of issues surrounding same-sex feelings and families are repositioned as a matter of civil rights rather than sex, teachers can begin to find ways to begin to create a more inclusive environment in which to discuss sexual minority issues. Teachers and drama practitioners can aid in this process by sharing age-appropriate resources and supplemental materials. However, because of the volatility of this issue, there is great controversy over the use of these resources with young people. How might concerned teachers and artists respond?

The lesson plans included in this chapter illustrate how a classroom teacher or drama practitioner can encourage young people to sensitively examine attitudes about same-sex feelings and families as a way to build awareness, empathy, and respect. Younger elementary students are introduced to Asha, who has problems at school when her two moms sign a permission slip for a field trip. In *Living in Secret,* older elementary students become involved in the story of a young girl who temporarily runs away with her mother and her mother's girlfriend. Should gay parents have the right to be awarded custody of their children?

The last part of the chapter lists several hands-on suggestions for teachers and practitioners who want to create an environment for equity in their classrooms or artistic work that respects a range of differences. The resources listed provide some useful springboards for further exploration through drama or theatre and can lead to spirited discussions about these vital issues.

Analyzing Assumptions About Sexual Orientation

In 1998, one of the most public and brutal killings of a young gay man occurred outside Laramie, Wyoming. Matthew Shepard was tied to a fence, severely beaten, and left to die. His only "crime" was being openly gay. The vehemence of this attack brought the harsh reality of homophobia in America to the public's attention as network anchors and newsmagazine programs scrutinized the incident. Debates resurfaced about the need for hate crime legislation. Yet a university student attending a vigil held in Matthew's memory held up a sign underscoring what is at the heart of the problem: "Attack Intolerance With Education" ("Lesson" 1998).

Sexual orientation is the one area of difference about which there is the greatest amount of intolerance in American culture. Heterosexuality is presumed to be the "norm" and is constantly reinforced throughout a young person's early experience of life and school. The popular media, including talk shows and movies, bombard young people with stereotypes and misperceptions about gay and lesbian people. Positive representations of same-sex feelings or same-sex families are virtually nonexistent in most classrooms or in popular culture in this country. Children struggling to make sense of their feelings and opinions about sexuality are often left confused. However, educators, theatre makers, and other caring adults can openly intervene and help students define and analyze the issues related to sexual orientation in positive age-appropriate ways.

Discriminatory Attitudes. Heterosexism can be defined as "a value-system that prizes heterosexuality, assumes it is the only appropriate manifestation of love and sexuality, and devalues homosexuality and all that is not heterosexual." (Herik 1989, 925). One of the most often articulated rationales against homosexuality is that it is biologically "unnatural" and therefore threatens an idealized notion of "family." Constructing homosexuality as unnatural, however, is directly related to how gender roles are constructed. Conservative understandings of gender roles tend to support this "preferred" or socially accepted view of sexuality. From an early age, gender role expectations underscore the "naturalness" of heterosexuality. As we mature, the careful construction of the "strong virile man" as the essential counterpart to the "delicate fertile woman" seamlessly adds up in the constructed equation of the heterosexual whole with its two "obvious" halves for procreation purposes.

Religious doctrines punctuate the "correctness" of this theorem. Same-sex couplings or feelings are therefore admonished, ridiculed, or considered "morally wrong." The *New York Times* recently reported that while Americans are generally more "tolerant" toward homosexuals than they were twenty-five years ago, 59 percent still believe it is morally wrong (Berke 1998). If someone is not fulfilling a perceived moral obligation and biological destiny and is instead changing the equation, so to speak, one could conclude that homosexuality has a negative impact on an idealized notion of "family;" such conclusions can lead to homophobic reactions.

Homophobia, or the fear of homosexuality that manifests itself in the desire or attempt to discriminate against gay or lesbian people, is often fueled by a lack of knowledge, which in turn gives greater credence to myths and fears. Reasons for homophobic feelings can include:

- a general fear of people who are different;
- an inability or unwillingness to change the hatred taught during childhood;
- strongly held religious beliefs or affiliations;
- revulsion at the thought of engaging in same-sex activity and generalizing that it must be wrong for everyone;
- low self-esteem leading to a need to hate others. ("Homophobia" 1999)

Although similar in scope to the reasons often cited to explain the racist and sexist behavior that multicultural education (MCE) literature seeks to redress, there are surprisingly few references that critique heterosexism or positively respond to issues of sexual orientation in the major MCE texts currently available on the market. As one of the few exceptions, Donna Gollnick and Philip Chin (1998) discuss homosexuality in their chapter on gender, although they cover the subject in a mere three pages. Following a discussion of gender discrimination, they stress that homophobia is another area of discrimination educators should be aware of, because there is still a large contingent that views homosexuality as either a sin, a sickness, or a crime (135). These supposedly tangible conditions, however, serve as nothing more than a smoke screen for a range of discriminatory attitudes about gays and lesbians.

The most virulent of these forms of discrimination posits gay and lesbian behavior as a sin. Many on the religious right have turned their fear into a crusade by attempting to convert gays and lesbians to heterosexuality and blaming their "lapse" in sexual judgment to the Devil's influence. Many fundamentalist Christian groups believe that through therapy, prayer, and the act of being "saved," gays and lesbians can become straight.[3] Using the Bible as a weapon, some fundamentalist Christians frequently cite passages that condemn "homosexual behavior" and doom offenders to Hell for defiance of "God's laws." Besides denying basic civil rights to a substantial sexual minority, the notion of deviance from what has been narrowly interpreted as "God's view" on the issue has effectively silenced any meaningful conversation about the religious or spiritual lives of gay and lesbian people. The question of how a democracy can accommodate and protect the right to religious differences as well as the rights of gay and lesbian people remains a troubling problem.

Another often-cited misperception about homosexuality involves the presumption of an evangelical aspect to sexual orientation and the belief that gays and lesbians are somehow involved in recruiting young people. This particularly noxious view is often used to discriminate against gay and lesbian teachers. While the repercussions of revealing sexual orientation in any job setting can be harmful if one is gay or lesbian, the reprisals in an educational environment can be devastating. Woods and Harbeck note that despite research regarding the inaccuracy of the assumption that gays and lesbians are "intensely" attracted to young people and try to "recruit" them to their "deviant lifestyle," this prejudicial view still has great appeal to heterosexists (1992, 142). The fact remains that while our views of sexuality are socially constructed, our sexual orientation is set fairly early in our maturation process. We are not, therefore, recruited to our sexual orientation—despite heterosexist constructions of the "workings" of homosexuality.

Dealing with the Facts. Since Kinsey's landmark study in 1948, which estimated 10 percent of the population to be homosexual, subsequent research and extrapolation provides a strong challenge to those of us who work with young people (Uribe and Harbeck 1992, 11). Consider the following facts:

- currently, an estimated 22 million people in the U.S. are gay or lesbian (Murphy 1992, 230);
- experts now agree that sexual orientation is not learned but is in place at an early age and is most probably determined by the ages of five or six (Harbeck 1992b, 127);
- gay and lesbian youth are coming out earlier than ever before, some as early as fifth or sixth grade (Rofes 1997b, xvi);
- if one out of ten people is gay, it is likely that two or three children in every K–6 school classroom are gay.

What are the implications of these facts for those of us who work in elementary classrooms or with elementary-aged students? A moment of classroom practice might help put these issues in perspective:

> A group of fifth graders is busy creating the circumstances surrounding a drama about a misunderstanding between two friends. After much discussion and some scene work we establish that Toni and her friend Jill are having problems. It seems that Jill has started some nasty rumors about Toni. As we are planning, one student suggests that the rumor had to do with Toni being gay. "Yeah," a usually reluctant student chimes in, "she's gay." There is an awkward pause. The girl playing Toni turns bright red and then glares at her classmate who made the comment. The teacher, who generally uses my time with her class to catch up on paperwork, slowly looks up, takes off her glasses, and gives everyone a hard look. Since I have only been working with this group for a short time, I still haven't sorted out the classroom dynamics—but something is definitely going on here that I don't quite understand—and it has something to do with Mary, the young woman playing Toni at the moment. I suddenly realize that this is the first time a gay issue has so overtly emerged in any of my elementary classroom drama work. Later the teacher will tell me that all the students have been teasing Mary about being gay. Still later Mary would tell me privately that she is kind of a tomboy and enjoys delivering papers with her dad every day. Eventually she tells me that everyone thinks she's gay. "I finally just stopped telling them to shut up," she says. "Instead, I told 'em all I *was* gay. I thought that would make 'em stop. But it hasn't."

Whether Mary is gay or not is not really the point; the response of the adults supposedly in charge of managing the situation is. A teacher doing nothing more than delivering harsh stares was not enough to guard against harassment. A drama practitioner doing nothing more than refocusing the group on "what else" might be troubling our fictional Toni and Jill was also a disservice to this harassed young woman who may be conflicted about her own emerging sense of sexual identity. We missed an opportunity to discuss substantive issues and directly challenge homophobic behavior.

Another key problem that emerges in Mary's story is the fact that many educators do not see elementary-aged students as possessing *any* kind of sexuality or sexual desire—much less a gay or lesbian one. This "missing discourse of desire," as Karen Libman (1998) points out, exacerbates the tensions and confusions young people feel about sexuality (58). These supposedly sexually-neutral beings are often not encouraged or given the opportunity to discuss sexuality in any kind of meaningful way. Yet sexual desires, feelings, and understandings begin to percolate even before young bodies start to change and develop. How do educators account for the fact that the onset of menstruation is occurring earlier than ever before with hormones becoming active as early as age nine (Pipher 1994, 53)? Yet many who work with young people often ignore these issues—not maliciously, but because of discomfort and a desire to hold on to an idealized notion of childhood that tends to construct young people as nonsexualized, innocent beings.

Responsible Interventions. Professional educators are charged with creating positive and safe learning environments for young people. Any form of harassment or discrimination needs to be responsibly confronted whenever it occurs in order to ensure that *all* students have the opportunity to learn, grow, and discover. Teachers and other adults serve as role models for what is considered acceptable behavior and our actions, comments, and attitudes exert great influence on how young people begin to make sense of the conflicting messages about acceptable ways to treat others.

One teacher shared a story with me about a six-year-old boy in her K–1 class who had very "flamboyant" mannerisms. He liked to dress up, and eventually some of the other students made fun of him. Instead of ignoring the situation, this teacher found ways to periodically comment about the world being made up of lots of different kinds of people who love each other in lots of different ways. "The most important thing is to be with people who treat you well," she would tell them. "It doesn't matter who it is. Just be with people who love you and treat you well." She also began to pull individual students aside and talked to them about supporting *all* their unique and wonderful classmates.

Curiously, parents often approach elementary teachers with concerns about their children's sexual orientation. Teachers have reported that parents of children as young as three or four years old have wondered, in particular, whether their child's dressing-up behavior was "normal" or not (Casper et al. 1996, 275). The word *normal* has troubling connotations in this regard and is loaded with less-than-positive implications about homosexuality. As educational researcher Elaine Wickens wonders:

> If it is normal for a six-year-old boy to dress in clothing of the other gender then he is okay, he is not gay. But, if he continues with this behavior in later years, then when is he no longer okay? When is it no longer normal? Do we imply by our language that being gay is abnormal? Do we also confuse questions of dressing in clothing of the other gender with questions of sexual orientation? (Casper et al., 277)

There is a delicate balance between how teachers handle these issues in the classroom with students and how they pacify parents outside the classroom.

A direct approach is often the best solution. Wickens notes a particularly sensitive and positive way one teacher responded to a mother's concern that her son might be gay because he liked to wear jewelry:

> First, we talked about seven-year-olds and their general interest in dressing up, fantasy play, and fidgeting with little plastic junk like toys, rings, hair barrettes, etc. I told her Ben was right on target in that area. Then I mentioned that wearing jewelry didn't mean that he was gay, but that one in ten people is gay, so it was likely that three children in our class are gay! She was a bit shocked. But if Ben is gay, she should start enjoying that fact ASAP! (Casper et al., 277)

This simple and direct approach is possible only if we have the courage to carefully examine our own prejudices and misperceptions and recognize how loaded words such as *normal* are in the context of sexuality. It also requires us to embrace the fact that gay and lesbian students are in our schools, classrooms, and drama workshops at this very moment— something that is not always easy to do.

Recently, I approached a friend who is an upper elementary teacher about possibly doing some drama with his students around sexual orientation issues, using some of the same-sex family story material outlined in the lesson plans later in this chapter. He shrugged his shoulders and said that there really was not a need for it in his school which is located in a low-income neighborhood with a large Latina/o population. Instead, he suggested that I try a school in a more liberal, upper-middle-class neighborhood because there was a greater likelihood that it would be an issue there. I was surprised. This is a teacher I admire, who is concerned about giving his students the tools necessary to succeed in school and in an economic system that tends to limit opportunities for Latinos. The leap required to connect those issues with other forms of discrimination such as homophobia is not always an easy one. Gay and lesbian students face some of the same problems as people with invisible disabilities: they are presumed not to exist unless there is an overt display of behavior or a "situation" occurs.

Teachers also need to be aware that language matters. The most widely used derogatory words in school today are versions of gay epithets: *fag, dyke, queer, sissy-boy,* along with expressions such as "That's so gay." If teachers choose to ignore this language, what are the consequences? Not to comment equals tacit agreement or compliance and sends a strong message to students that gay-bashing is acceptable. Teachers need to be vigilant and insistent about protecting the rights of all their students. They may be uncomfortable about dealing with gay and lesbian issues or conflicted about their feelings concerning homosexuality, but it is their responsibility to provide the leaders of tomorrow with an understanding of respect for a range of individual differences.

The Controversy over Resources. There are several resources and organizations available to aid teachers in their attempts to create a climate of understanding and respect for issues related to sexual orientation. However, many of these resources have been hotly contested. For example, *It's Elementary* was widely denounced by conservative religious groups, who typically referred to it as a "dangerous video" that promotes a "lifestyle condemned by all the world's major religions" ("Unacceptable!" 1997). Likewise, the National Education Association has been denounced for its resolution supporting tolerance and acceptance of gay and lesbian issues in schools. Groups such as the conservative Concerned Women of America (CWA), who launched a rigorous campaign to promote a "pro-family" agenda that condemns teaching young people that "gay is OK," have had a troubling impact on the availability and use of resources (Rofes 1997a).

Several controversies have erupted over various picture books and novels for young readers. In Canada, a bitter dispute broke out in 1998 between teachers and their school board concerning three picture books that were to be incorporated into a K–1 curriculum on families. The school board eventually banned the books from being used in any schools in their district. The books in question included *Asha's Mums, Belinda's Bouquet,* and *One Dad, Two Dads, Brown Dads, Blue Dads,* all depicting same-sex families in sensitive but nonexplicit ways. The words *gay, lesbian, homosexual,* or *sex* do not appear in any of these stories. Concerned parents, students, and teachers brought a lawsuit to the British Columbia Supreme Court, which resulted in the overturning of the school board's ban by the higher court (Joyce 1998).

Closer to home a nasty incident occurred in Wichita Falls, Texas, in May 1998, when religious leaders asked the city council to ban two children's books, *Heather Has Two Mommies* and *Daddy's Roommate.* One book tells the story of a girl who has two lesbian mothers while the other focuses on the relationship between a boy, his gay father, and his father's boyfriend. Both books have been the target of controversy from members of the religious right since they were published.[4]

This particular controversy, initially sparked by Pastor Robert Jeffress, centered on objections to the local library's use of public funding to "sanction" literature that he felt promoted a homosexual lifestyle. In what he saw as an act of civil disobedience, Jeffress checked out the books and refused to return them. He was very clear concerning his objections about the books, *Daddy's Roommate* in particular. "What many Christians object to is that the book promotes sodomy," Jeffress said. "It has a picture of two men in bed together. We object to sodomy because it is against the law, and is responsible for the greatest epidemic in history. AIDS is a gay disease that has spilled over into our society." While it's true that *Daddy's Roommate* shows a picture of two men in bed, one sleeping, the other turning out a bedside light, the book contains no sexually explicit material. The shock of this kind of bigotry illustrates the ease with which many on the religious right have conveniently explained away the need for responsible action toward AIDS and those affected by it.

Jeffress encouraged sympathetic community members to join in a letter-writing campaign designed to bombard the local paper with public support for banning the books. While these letters typically quoted the Bible to support their positions and were often vehement in their opinions about the "sin" of homosexuality, none of the letters referenced anything of substance concerning the actual books in question.

From the outset of the controversy, Wichita Falls Public Library administrator Linda Hughes pointed out that the library chose these books from the American Library Association's best book list, which is overseen by psychologists, sociologists, and educators. Hughes noted that they were the first children's books the library had ever carried that depicted gay families and that they were chosen because of their gentle and honest treatment of alternate family structures. Interestingly, as the controversy wore on, fifteen community members volunteered to replace the books with their own money (Quin 1998).

Finally, on June 24, 1998, the issue was addressed by the Wichita Falls Library Advisory Board (appointed by the city council), who voted to keep the books but to move them to different locations in the library (Hundley 1998). Hughes' choice to move the texts out of the picture book section of the library to the juvenile social sciences area, which houses other literature on family issues, seemed to strike a chord of happy compromise for liberals who were supportive but not completely comfortable with the material. However, Jeffress and cohorts were not pleased with this decision and leveled threats at individual board members who supported the books as well as at several members of the City Council, vowing to "vote out the infidels who would deny God and his word" (Zollo 1998).

At the heart of controversies such as these are several questions: How do teachers who are committed to recognizing and honoring diversity deal with the considerable forces that oppose such explorations? How do we vigilantly protect the civil rights of all our citizens—gay and lesbian *and* Christian without compromising a firm belief in respect for difference? Both of the incidents described above could have resulted in teachers, librarians, and local citizens deferring to the homophobic assumptions imbedded in each of the protests against the literature in question. However, in both instances a final judgment based on a commitment to civil rights, respect, and an appreciation of diversity prevailed. The lesson here is significant: Do not assume that discussing issues of respect for all members of society, including gays and lesbians, is off limits just because you may be in a conservative context. James Chamberlain (1999), the teacher who sparked the book-banning controversy in British Columbia, encourages teachers everywhere to boldly use the age-appropriate resources available to aid in the struggle to eliminate homophobia and prejudice from schools. In his words, "Every child's future and ability to learn depends upon it!"

"It's Not About Sex!" I recently asked a young lesbian what misperceptions she thought heterosexuals had about gays and lesbians. "That it's our choice," she said immediately, "and that it's all about sex! It's *not* about sex!" She went on to eloquently talk about her own experience growing up gay. "People think you're a freak. You have no laws to protect you, you can't keep a job, you have to worry about being harassed, you can't adopt a child in most states. But if you break up with the person you've loved, your heart is broken—just like a heterosexual."

As teachers and drama practitioners try to maneuver carefully through the land mines that are ever present when considering how to discuss gay and lesbian issues with young people, one thing is clear. The reason to address these issues has nothing to do with sex. Instead, adopting a pluralistic perspective in our work demands that we concern ourselves with finding ways to help young people appreciate and respect diverse kinds of relationships, to question bias and the kinds of discrimination that can surface when people do not respect or appreciate others, and to realize how discrimination can affect real people.

"You know, nobody fits into a box," my friend told me later in our conversation. "There is no one box out there. I just want to tell kids: Be who you are. Accept who you are." It's something she wished someone had told her when she was young. As much as some conservative religious groups and nervous administrators would like to deny it, schools are not "gay-free" entities. A healthy education helps young people learn to respect a range of differences—including various orientations to sexuality—others' and their own.

Building Awareness

The following lesson plans are designed to illustrate how a classroom teacher or drama practitioner can engage young people in the examination of situations involving same-sex families as a way to begin to build awareness and respect for gay and lesbian issues in age-appropriate ways.

TOPIC: SEXUAL ORIENTATION—GAY/LESBIAN FAMILIES

Focus How does a young girl convince her school that she really *does* have two moms?

Teaching Objectives

To consider stereotypes and preconceptions that many people have about gays and lesbians;

To explore the issues that confront children of gay and lesbian families;

To reflect on and discuss how to take action against those stereotypes.

Target Age K–3rd grade

Time Needed One 45-minute session

Materials

- Picture book depicting different family structures such as *Families: A Celebration of Diversity, Commitment and Love* by Alyette Jenness (Houghton Mifflin, 1990) or *Who's in a Family* by Robert Skutch (Berkeley, CA: Tricycle Press, 1994)
- *Asha's Mums* by Rosamund Elwin and Michele Paulse (Toronto: Women's Press, 1990). Asha almost misses a class field trip because her teacher will only accept her biological mother's signature on the permission slip. The incident escalates as curious classmates tease her about having two moms but then reveal their own diverse family situations.

Procedure

1. ENGAGE the students: Show students several pictures that depict different family configurations. Ask the students: *What do these pictures have in common? How are they different? One thing they have in common is that they are all pictures of different kinds of families. There are many types of families. What is a family?* (A group of people living under one roof with one or more adults who care for each other and any children that may live there, too.) *No two families are exactly alike. They are all different and unique. We all have different people in our families depending on who we are. If there was a picture of your family here, who would we see? Who makes up your unique family?* (Give students the

Figure 5–3. Asha's Mums *by Rosamund Elwin and Michele Paulse.*

opportunity to talk about their various family situations.) *Let's look at story that focuses on a girl who is having trouble convincing her friends and teacher about her unique family.*

2. SHARE the story: Gather students in close and read *Asha's Mums.* Pause to discuss various illustrations. For example: *What seems to be going on? How do you know? How might people be feeling? Why might they feel that way? What would you do if you were Asha? The teacher? Her friend? Her biological mom?*
3. EXPLORE the story:
   a. Narrative pantomime: Ask the students to find a space in the room and to imagine that they are all students in Asha's class. *You have just put on your school clothes but are still sleepy and realize what you really need is a great b-i-g stretch. You stretch out your arms and your legs until you are standing on your tiptoes with your fingers trying to touch the ceiling. Then you drop down and touch your toes and then you stretch back up again making yourself as big and tall as you can. Now, imagine that you are in the bathroom and you turn on the water*

and wash your face. You remember to scrub your ears! You turn off the water and grab a fluffy towel and dry off your face. Next you pick up your toothbrush, put toothpaste on it very carefully, add a little bit of water, and you brush your teeth—each and every one of them. You take a drink of water and spit it out. Rinse out the sink. And now you are all ready to go. You pick up your backpack and check it once last time. Where is your permission slip for the field trip? Hum. There it is! You put on your backpack and are all ready for school!

b. Image work: Ask the students to image that someone took a photograph of Asha and all of her classmates in class as they are getting ready to hand in their permission slips. Discuss how they might organize themselves if they were to create that picture. Ask for one student to volunteer to be Asha and ask students where she should be sitting. Count to three and ask the students to freeze perfectly still as they get ready to hand in their forms. Remind them that the only things they are allowed to move are their eyelashes while they are frozen. Comment on their facial expressions and body positions. Let the group relax and then ask them to imagine how they might react when the teacher tells Asha that her form is not correct. Ask how Asha might react. On a three-count ask students to freeze into this picture. Comment on the differences you see in their faces and bodies.

c. Discussion: *How do you think Asha felt when the teacher said her form was not correctly filled out? Sometimes we think things that we do not say out loud. What do you think might have been going through her mind? What might her classmates think about Asha and her family? How do you think her teacher feels? Why do you suppose they feel that way? What advice would you give Asha about what she should do? Let's see what Asha and her classmates might talk about during recess.*

d. Teacher in role: The teacher takes on the role of Asha and asks for advice. *What am I supposed to do? I really do have two moms. I'm not lying. Some people think that's it's weird, but I don't. What do you think I should do? I really want to go to the science center!* Prompt students to list ideas, combine as needed, and work to prioritize what seems to be the top two or three ways she can convince the teacher that her form is correct.

e. Scene work: Depending on age and previous drama experience, either have the whole group work together to convince the teacher to take Asha's form *or* divide into groups to play out their suggestions from the previous activity. After the scene(s), discuss: *How did it go?*

Did Asha get what she wanted? Why or why not? What else could she do? Try other suggestions if there is time.

4. REFLECT on the issues: *Why do you suppose some people were confused about Asha's family? How do you think that made her feel? What can she do about that? How can other people help?*
5. EVALUATE the lesson: What did you notice about the group's willingness to discuss this issue? Was there any reluctance to engage? If so, why? What stereotypes were brought up? How do you feel you handled them? How did the students respond to Asha's dilemma? What things still need to be examined? What questions did you have trouble answering? Which discussion sections worked best? Why? What do students seem most interested in concerning this issue? Based on your evaluation, how might you follow up this lesson?

Possible Extensions

Language Arts

- Write a story or draw a set of pictures telling the story of one of the families discussed in *Asha's Mums*.
- Discuss strategies for persuading someone to do something. List three ideas that seem to work.
- Write a note to Asha telling her how you feel about what happened.

Art

Make a collage of your own family.

Social Studies

Make a map of your neighborhood and all the different families that live there.

TOPIC: SEXUAL ORIENTATION—CIVIL RIGHTS

Focus Should gay parents be allowed to have custody of their children?

Teaching Objectives

To consider stereotypes and preconceptions that many people have about gays and lesbians;

To explore the issues that confront gay and lesbian families;

To reflect on and discuss how to take action against those stereotypes.

Target Age 4th–6th grade

Time Needed Two 45-minute sessions

Materials

- *Living in Secret* by Cristina Salat (Orinda, CA: Books MarcUs, 1999). After a difficult divorce, the court has ordered that eleven-year-old Amelia is to live with her father and only be allowed limited contact with her lesbian mother. Amelia and her mother decide to run away and live in secret until a private detective finds them. Amelia is forced to go back to her father's house.
- Note 1: "Dear Daddy, I am running away from home. I love you, but I don't want to live with you anymore. You're never home and Rosa is always on the phone with friends. You don't need me around. Don't worry about me; I'll be fine. Love, Amy."
- Note 2: "A: We are going to San Francisco. I've rented a house for us. It has a backyard. Your mother said you can get a cat or dog, if you want. Do you have any questions? J."

Procedure

1. ENGAGE the students: Ask the students how many in the group feel that they might be a good detective. *What skills would someone need in order to be a good detective?* (Possible skills include: curiosity, observation skills, ability to decide what is important evidence, ability to make connections between the case and the information gathered, etc.) Invite the students to "think like detectives" for a few minutes. Show them the first note and ask someone to read it out loud. Ask what facts the group can glean from the note and what questions the note leaves them with. Record their impressions. Show and read the second note. Ask what new information this note provides and what new questions it brings up.
2. SHARE the source material: Drawing on their conclusions and questions, explain that an eleven-year-old girl named Amelia has run away from home. Six years earlier, Amelia's parents got divorced and the court decreed that she had to live with her wealthy father and could only have limited contact with her mother, who is a lesbian. Amy (as her dad called her) was heartbroken and missed her mom very much. Although they were able to see each other occasionally, she and her mom vowed they would live together again somehow. Between her father's work schedule, which included a lot of travel, and his new girlfriend, Rosa, Amy grew to hate living with her dad.

Finally, a plan evolved for Amy, her mom, and her mom's girlfriend, Janey, to run away to California and live in secret under assumed names. Everything was going well; Amelia was making friends and had a tutor to help her keep up with her studies, and her mom and Janey both had jobs. But one year later, a private detective hired by her father found them. Amy's dad decided not to press kidnapping charges if Amy promised to leave with him immediately. As much as she didn't want to leave she also did not want her mother and Janey to go to jail. It wasn't that she didn't love her dad. She just wanted to live with her Mom and Janey and could not understand why her mom had been denied custody. *Was the judge prejudiced? Should gay parents have the right to have custody of their children? What happens when what a child wants is different from what the court or other adults want?*

3. EXPLORE the source material:

   a. Scene work: In small groups, ask students to create one scene from a moment in Amelia's adventure. Possible scenes include:

      - divorce courtroom—Dad gets custody
      - at home—Amy with Dad and Rosa
      - at the airport—Amy in disguise with Mom and Janey
      - at the beach—a new life with friends and family
      - at the California house—the detective finds them
      - at the airport—Amy's dad takes her away

   Share the scenes and discuss what new information we learn after each showing.

   b. Discussion: Mention that after Amelia was taken away from her mom in California, she faced a big decision. As she saw it, she had three choices: 1. run away again, 2. stay with her dad until she was eighteen, or 3. go back to court and fight another custody battle, this time adding her voice to the mix. *If you were Amelia, what would you do? What do you think she should do?* Discuss and list the pros and cons of each choice.

   c. Court video: Ask students to imagine what might have happened if her family had gone through a second custody battle. *Based on the information presented in the above scenes, who might testify? What kinds of things would they say? What other kinds of professionals might be in favor of joint custody? Who might be against Amelia's mother having custody?* Create a list and then ask students to work in pairs or small groups to craft a statement by one of those people who might testify or create a dialogue between a lawyer and the person testifying. (The list might include: Amelia, Mom, Janey, Dad, Rosa, grandparents, friends, school counselor, teacher, social worker, doctor, neighbors, religious leaders, and others.)

Frame the sharing of the scenes as if the observers are members of the press who have been allowed to view a series of videotaped statements or interactions. The members of the press can take notes as needed. Play all the court "videos" and then discuss them out of role. *Which statements seemed most compelling? Why? What questions does this leave the press with?*

d. The press reports: Let students decide how the press would report on this case. Individually or in small groups have students create video reports or written stories. Show "video clips" and post written stories for everyone to read.

e. A verdict: After reviewing the testimony and the press reports, ask students to imagine that they are the judge in this case. What would they decide about Amy's situation? How would they justify that decision? Have students write down their verdict and justification. Tally their verdicts and discuss the various reasons cited.

f. Scene work: Create an image of a courtroom scene just prior to the judge's handing down of the verdict the majority of the class voted for. On a signal, activate the scene and run it up until the point that the verdict has been spoken. Freeze it again and ask students to identify any thoughts their characters might be thinking. Tap different characters on the shoulder and have them speak their thoughts. Replay with other verdicts if useful.

4. REFLECT on the issues: *What kinds of attitudes about gays and lesbians did Amelia and her mom encounter? Why do you suppose people have those kinds of attitudes? What will it take to help change other people's attitudes about the rights of gay and lesbian people?*

5. EVALUATE the lesson: What did you notice about the group's willingness to discuss this issue? Was there any reluctance to engage? If so, why? What stereotypes were brought up? How do you feel you handled them? How did the students respond to the discussion of gay rights? What things still need to be examined? What questions did you have trouble answering? Which discussion segments worked best? Why? What do students seem most interested in concerning this issue? Based on your evaluation, how might you follow up this lesson?

Possible Extensions

Language Arts

Create the police and/or detective report about the case.

Social Studies

Look at how court procedures in custody cases actually unfold. Combine this inquiry with a field trip to a courtroom or invite a judge to speak about how he or she makes decisions about difficult cases.

Health

Examine how to make a good decision and create a list of at least five suggestions on how to make "healthy choices."

Creating an Environment for Equity

How can we teach with an awareness of the impact of overt *and* covert heterosexist assumptions? Whether you are an educator seeking to create an inclusive learning environment or a theatre practitioner striving to create artistic work that is responsive to diversity, here are several suggestions for including attention to issues of sexuality in your work:

- Be aware that conservative notions of gender and gender roles often lead to conservative views about sexuality.
- Remember that heterosexuality is not universal.
- Keep in mind the fact that schools are not "gay-free" zones and that you are working with young people who are beginning to come to terms with their own sexuality; at least 10 percent of the students you are working with may be gay or lesbian.
- Be aware of the impact of language and how it helps shape views and attitudes about sexuality. Confront gay epithets when they occur.
- As you create lesson plans or theatre work for young people, ask yourself what might be learned or implied about sexuality in this lesson or performance piece.
- Recognize the unwitting ways heterosexism is reinforced in classroom interactions or play scripts. For example, avoid deliberately placing students in stereotypical nuclear family groups. Let students experiment with different kinds of family groupings.

- When gay characters are constructed in drama/theatre work, consider the impact of the characterization. Many "over the top" representations are exploited for comic value and tend to reinforce negative stereotypes. Develop ways to talk about this with the students you work with.
- Look for opportunities to tie respect for sexual differences to basic civil rights issues.
- Openly confront issues and problems when they come up. However, don't wait for them to "just come up." Be proactive!

Questions to Ponder

1. How would you describe your own orientation to sexuality? When were you first made aware of societal expectations regarding sexuality? How have those expectations affected you?
2. How do expectations about sexuality affect the students you ordinarily interact with? What tensions does sexual orientation cause between students? How comfortable would a gay or lesbian student be in this environment? How does *your* sexual orientation affect your work with students? What incidents have caused you to notice tensions? What can be done to help alleviate these tensions?
3. To what degree is sexual orientation an issue in your workplace? How much openness and acceptance of gays and lesbians is there in your work environment? How comfortable is it to be gay or lesbian in your workplace? What can be done to increase respect for the rights of gay and lesbian coworkers in your working environment?
4. While some educators strongly believe that discussing gay and lesbian issues in the classroom is a logical component of a comprehensive multicultural curriculum, teachers often find themselves at odds with upper administration. Penalties are often severe—ranging from harsh reprimands to the termination of employment. How should educators and artists committed to equity issues proceed? Is it worth the risk to discuss gay and lesbian issues in the classroom?
5. On the national level, resources on gay issues for educators, such as the video *It's Elementary,* have been targeted by conservative organizations such as the Eagle Forum as one of the ways in which schools are channeling funds into "teaching homosexuality" instead of strengthening traditional classroom teaching methods and upholding "family values." How might a committed artist-teacher counter such claims?

Practical Problems to Consider

1. Working with a retelling of *Sleeping Beauty* as a source for creative drama or theatre work, how would you structure the work so that the presumption of heterosexuality is examined or at least questioned?
2. You are working with a group of fourth-grade students who are busily dramatizing various scenes inspired by *The Frog Prince* in small groups. As you check on each group's progress, you overhear several homophobic comments from a group of boys who are supposed to be working on the kissing scene. How do you respond?
3. During the sharing of improvisational scenes based on occupations, a group of third-graders have created a hair salon and included a stereotypical gay character which prompts a good deal of laughter from the other students. How do you respond?
4. A second-grade colleague wants to approach the topic of gay families with her class but is not sure how to best proceed. How might you help her create an activity or lesson plan that positively values same-sex family situations?
5. After conducting a drama lesson using *Asha's Mums* as source material, you receive a complaint from a parent who has asked for a meeting to discuss this story and the dramatization with you. How do you handle the situation? What rationale do you give for your choice of source material and subject matter?

A Case Study Situation

A fifth-grade team of teachers has been given permission by upper administration to include gay and lesbian civil rights as part of a larger unit on the U.S. Constitution and the Bill of Rights. The principal feels this is consistent with the district's current initiatives to infuse multicultural and antiracist content across the curriculum. Since the team is concerned that students may feel uncomfortable about these issues or not take them seriously, you have been contacted as a consultant on how they might use drama or theatre work to fully engage students in the topic. How do you proceed? What kinds of activities might you suggest?

You are invited to help report on the team's progress at the next faculty meeting. After the report, some other teachers raise several questions about the appropriateness of this subject matter at the elementary level. A constant theme is that the students are too young to think about "these things." One colleague insists that homosexuality should not be considered part of the district's multicultural agenda because the issues are completely different from the reality of race and racial bias. Questions are also raised about the need for parental consent before talking about gay issues in the classroom. How do you respond to these concerns? How do you justify addressing this subject matter in this way at the fifth-grade level?

Resources for Drama and Theatre Work on Same-sex Issues

Picture Books

Daddy's Roommate by M. Willhoite (Boston: Alyson Publications, 1991). A boy describes life with his father and his father's partner.

Heather Has Two Mommies by Leslea Newman (Boston: Alyson Publications, 1989). A girl sees nothing unusual about having two moms in this realistic treatment of lesbian parenting. Includes information about artificial insemination.

Lucy Goes to the Country by Joseph Kennedy (Los Angeles: Alyson Publications, 1998). A gay couple and their cat spend an adventurous weekend in the country.

One Dad, Two Dads, Brown Dads, Blue Dads by Johnny Valentine (Boston: Alyson Press, 1994). A boy talks about life with his two "blue" dads in this rhyming story.

The Duke Who Outlawed Jellybeans and Other Stories by Johnny Valentine (Boston: Alyson Press, 1991). Collection of short stories depicting a variety of family situations. Title story is a lovely allegory about accepting difference.

Older Readers

Earthshine by Theresa Nelson (New York: Bantam Doubleday Dell, 1994). A girl struggles with her father's AIDS-related illness and develops a closer bond with his partner.

No Big Deal by Ellen Jaffe McClain (New York: Puffin Books, 1997). A young teen takes action when her mother tries to get her favorite teacher fired because of rumors about his sexual orientation.

The Method by Paul Robert Walker (San Diego, CA: Harcourt Brace, 1997). Fifteen-year-old Albie enrolls in a summer acting class and gains insight on sexual expression and identity.

The Skull of Truth by Bruce Coville (San Diego, CA: Harcourt Brace, 1997). Charlie finds a skull that forces people to tell the truth and learns, among other things, that his uncle's roommate is his boyfriend.

Plays

Cootie Shots by Fringe Benefits Theatre Company under the direction of Norma Bowles, Artistic Director. An engaging collection of dramatic and musical vignettes about a range of diversity issues, including ethnicity, gender, sexual orientation, class, and ability. (For more information, contact Fringe Benefits Theatre Company, P.O. Box 691215, West Hollywood, CA 90069; 310-657-8149; e-mail: <normabowles@earthlink.net>.)

Five Good Resources for Drama and Theatre Work on Same-sex Families and Feelings

A Safe Place for Questions by Barbara Blinick. A terrific series of lesson ideas on gay and lesbian issues designed for grades 1–12. Begins with discussions about families and respect for difference in the elementary grades, moving to name-calling and stereotyping at the middle school level, and homophobia and history of sexuality for high school students. From San Francisco Unified School District's Support Services for Gay and Lesbian Youth, 1997. (For more information, contact School Health Programs Department, SFUSD, 1512 Golden Gate Avenue, San Francisco, CA 94115; 415-749-3400.)

Coming Out of the Classroom Closet: Gay and Lesbian Students, Teachers, and Curricula edited by Karen Harbeck. An excellent resource for examining a variety of issues related to gay and lesbian issues and schools. Vital for educators who want to confront homophobia in their classrooms. From Harrington Park Press, 10 Alice Street, Binghamton, NY 13904-1580.

Gay, Lesbian and Straight Education Network (GLSEN). GLSEN is a national organization that, according to their mission statement, "strives to assure that each member of every school community is valued and respected, regardless of sexual orientation." They suggest discussion topics, lesson plan ideas, and provide easy access to relevant news articles. (For more information, contact their website: <http://www.glsen.org>.)

It's Elementary: Talking About Gay Issues in School video documentary by Debra Chasnoff and Helen Cohen. Excellent video resource for educators about addressing gay stereotypes in age-appropriate ways at the elementary and middle school level. From Women's Educational Media, 1997. (For more information, contact Women's Educational Media, 2180 Bryant Street, Suite 203, San Francisco, CA 94110. 415-641-4616; website: <http://www.womedia.org>.)

Love Makes a Family: Lesbian, Gay, Bisexual and Transgender People and Their Families and *In Our Family: Portraits of All Kinds of Families.* Traveling photo-text exhibits for K–12 and adults. (For more information, contact Family Diversity Projects, P.O. Box 1209, Amherst, MA 01004. 413-256-0502; e-mail: <famphoto@javanet.com>; website: <http://www.familydiv.org>.)

Notes

1. While this exercise is an engaging way to begin conversations about the connection between basic civil rights and blatant prejudice against gays and lesbians, it should be acknowledged that the argument for marriage is controversial within the gay and lesbian community partly due to assimilationist concerns.

2. For more information, see "The Employment Non-Discrimination Act (ENDA)." *Human Rights Campaign Home Page.* 19 October 1999 <http://www.hrc.org/issues/leg/enda/index.html>.

3. See the *Religious Tolerance Home Page* (http://www.religioustolerance.org/hom_fuel.htm) for more information on conservative Christian attitudes about sexual orientation.

4. Details of this particular controversy have been summarized from Monica Wolfson's newspaper article "Books under fire: Religious leaders denounce gay stories," from the Wichita Falls *Times Record News Online.* See <http://www.wtr.com/html/5_16_98.htm>.

6

Disorienting Abilities

what is "normal"?

[E]mpathy for the disabled is unavailable to most able-bodied persons. Sympathy, yes, empathy, no, for every attempt to project oneself into that condition, to feel what it is like not to be ambulatory, for instance, is mediated by an ability to walk.

—SUE HALPERN, REVIEW OF *UNDER THE EYE OF THE CLOCK, NEW YORK TIMES REVIEW OF BOOKS.*

It was the first time I'd ever had an argument with a Deaf person.[1] While working with an outreach team to create a teachers' resource packet for UT's production of Suzan Zeder's play *Mother Hicks,* I discovered that the final version of the twenty-four-page packet had provoked a very strong reaction from Gene Mirus, a Deaf actor playing the character named Tuc, a young man who is cast out by his community because of his deafness. Gene asked to see me. He was particularly concerned about our section on American Sign Language (ASL). "You don't understand," he told me through an interpreter, "ASL is *not* just another form of English! It's more than what you say in here."

The section devoted to sign language focused mostly on finger spelling exercises and how to sign a sentence in ASL using standard English grammar. We had already printed the packets and were getting ready to send them to teachers. I had a million other things to do and I wanted to cross this off my list. And, besides, we were only trying to provide a *brief* introduction to the idea of sign language—nothing more.

"How should we have represented it, then?" I asked, trying to honor his concern but put this incident in the past. Gene was straightforward with me. Although he could tell that the last thing I wanted was to regroup the team and have them redo the packet, he did *not* want the current information to go out to the teachers of the several hundred schoolchildren who were already booked to see the show.

It was then that he began to "voice," something he rarely does. "ASL is its own language," he began in the hollow tones of one whose primary mode of communication is not oral, but he was determined to make me understand. "It's not English! It has its own grammar and syntax. It's the language of Deaf culture. Deaf people cherish being Deaf, they cherish their community and American Sign Language."

I finally realized that we really had made a big mistake. And I was profoundly embarrassed. I ordinarily thought of myself as a culturally sensitive person yet, in this case, I had completely ignored the cultural dynamics of the Deaf community. But even worse, I had not rigorously challenged my students to think about these issues either. In the process, I had unwittingly passed on a limiting understanding of ability in favor of uncritical experiments with finger spelling and a surface encounter with ASL as nothing more than signed English. Needless to say, we changed the copy and reprinted the packet. I am still grateful to Gene for making me painfully aware of the ingrained assumptions and misperceptions people who live their lives as "abled" have toward those whom they consider "disabled." How do these misperceptions sneak into our drama classrooms and theatre work? What can we do to openly address them? What do "people with no known disabilities" need to be aware of as they work with and represent people with disabilities?[2]

ABC's of Ability

In the world of "norms" we inhabit, in which everything seems to be measured against some kind of mean or average (think about blood pressure, weight, SAT scores, and other measurements), the body's basic abilities are no exception. An understanding of disability, as disability studies scholar Leonard Davis points out, is measured against what is considered "normal." Davis (1997) asserts that "normalcy is constructed to create the 'problem' of the disabled person" (9). My analysis of ability will focus on how the "problem" of disability has been constructed by mainstream U.S. culture and the impact of these often limiting constructions.

Building understanding about bias towards people with disabilities involves openly discussing physical and cognitive difference and the ways in which societal attitudes contribute to limiting achievement. In the lesson plans included in this chapter, younger elementary students are introduced to

Oliver, an octopus with a physical disability who shares his experience of the world. Older elementary students puzzle over how negative assumptions about cognitive disabilities, such as dyslexia, affect a young woman's progress in school and her sense of self.

Creating an environment in which there is an awareness of ability as well as a sensitivity to the rhetoric of disability can help teachers continue to openly discuss, work with, and represent a variety of abilities in their theatre and drama work. As educators and theatre makers we can help transform the language of disability into a language of possibility as we rethink our practice and pedagogy through our awareness of what people are able to accomplish instead of what they "lack."

Analyzing Ability

Consider a group of people with the following physical conditions:

- a woman who has a recurring knee injury
- a man who is extremely shy
- a woman who is experiencing difficulty reading the small print she used to read easily
- a man who periodically has chronic lower back pain
- a woman who is hearing impaired and communicates through American Sign Language
- a man who has muscular dystrophy and uses a wheelchair

If, as the U.S. Bureau of the Census (1997) defines it, having a disability means a person experiences "difficulty performing certain functions, or has difficulty performing the activities of daily living, or has difficulty with certain social roles," which of these people has a disability? It would seem that they *all* would experience difficulty in at least one of these areas. However, which of these people would you label as "disabled"? Identity perceptions shift significantly at the mention of this term. What are the connotations associated with this label? How are economic conditions affected by these "disabilities"? For example, of the people listed above, who should be entitled to public assistance? Who should be entitled to protection under the 1990 Americans with Disabilities Act (ADA), which safeguards the civil rights of people with disabilities? If, for instance, having a severe disability means a person is unable to perform one or more activities, uses an assistive device to help with mobility, or requires another person to help them with basic daily activities, which of these people has a severe disability? These are difficult questions. Based on the assumptions and misperceptions associated with the terms *ability* and *disability*, how do we individually and culturally construct and represent what it means to be "disabled"?

Constructing Dis/ability. The experience of daily life is, by and large, organized around the expectation that individuals can move their arms and legs in particular kinds of ways, can utilize five senses, and can reason in an accepted manner. The world is structured, as feminist scholar Susan Wendell (1997) points out, "for people who have no weaknesses" (260). According to recent U.S. Bureau of the Census (1997) documents, approximately one in five Americans has some kind of disability. One in ten has a severe disability. The rest of the population could be considered "temporarily abled."[3] As we age, our hearing, vision, mobility, and mental capacities change or are compromised—a fact that most people who are temporarily abled do not like to admit. If we are involved in any kind of accident or mishap, the process can be accelerated. An estimated 85 percent of people with disabilities were not born with them but acquired them later in life (Shapiro 1993).

Most definitions of disability are from an able-bodied perspective in which the body is assumed to be "intact" or "normal." For example, the United Nations and World Health Organization make the following distinctions:

> Impairment: Loss or abnormality of psychological, physiological or anatomical structure or function.
>
> Disability: Any restriction or lack of ability to perform an activity in the manner or within the range considered normal for a human being.
>
> Handicap: A disadvantage for a given individual resulting from an impairment or a disability that limits or prevents the fulfillment of a role that is normal depending on age, sex, social and cultural factors for that individual. (Quoted in Wendell 1997, 262)

While acknowledging that these definitions are framed by the complex political agendas of these two organizations, their construction of what is considered normal (and what is not) is striking.

The prevailing presumption of "able-bodiedness" puts people with disabilities at a distinct disadvantage in the social realm. Like *racism* and *sexism, ableism* is a catch-all term; it is used to describe everything from the belief that people with disabilities are inferior to people who have no known disabilities to blatant discrimination, exclusion, and victimization based on ability (Ellis and Llewellyn 1997, 113). Ableist assumptions often limit access to education, jobs, housing, and basic public services and can severely affect quality of life.

Despite the devastating effects of ableist assumptions, ability has not been as rigorously theorized as a site of oppression as other facets of identity such as race, class, and gender. For many, there is an assumption that disability is subsumed in race, class, and gender and therefore does not need to be considered as a separate category.[4] However, Leonard Davis (1997) points out that, if the census statistics are accurate, people with disabilities constitute the largest physical minority group in the country. In his words:

> Put another way, there are more people with disabilities than there are African-Americans or Latinos. But why have the disabled been rendered more invisible than other groups? Why are issues about perception, mobility, accessibility, distribution of bio-resources, physical space, difference not seen as central to the human condition? (2)

Because disability often evokes a complex mixture of emotions including sympathy for the "afflicted," gratefulness that *your* body is intact, and relief in distancing most disabilities as pathological problems under the domain of medicine, most people with no known disabilities perceive themselves as having no stake in the issues related to ability. However, as Davis (1995) asserts:

> Disability is not an object—a woman with a cane—but a social process that intimately involves everyone who has a body and lives in the world of senses. Just as the conceptualization of race, class, and gender shapes the lives of those who are not black, poor, or female, so the concept of disability regulates the bodies of those who are "normal." (2)

As a regulated social process, the construction of "disability" as "less than" is like any other form of oppression. In this instance, deeply held beliefs about the ideal body by an "ableist"-centered culture systematically discriminate and limit access and possibility. Susan Wendell (1996) elaborates:

> disability is "socially constructed" by such factors as social conditions that cause or fail to prevent damage to people's bodies; expectation of performance; the physical and social organization of societies on the basis of a young, non-disabled, "ideally shaped," healthy adult male paradigm of citizens; the failure or unwillingness to create ability among citizens who do not fit the paradigm; and cultural representations, failures of representation, and expectations. Much, but perhaps not all, of what can be socially constructed can be socially (and not just intellectually) deconstructed, given the means and the will. (45)

Material Concerns. The economic impact of the various social processes that limit possibilities and access based on ability is one of the most devastating effects of this form of discrimination. Despite the passing of the Americans with

Disabilities Act in 1990, which attempted to improve access and eliminate bias against people with disabilities, the U.S. Bureau of the Census (1994) reports that while employment opportunities are gradually increasing, people with disabilities constitute only 13 percent of the employed. Interestingly, only one-quarter of Americans with disabilities aged twenty-two to sixty-four receive any public assistance (U.S. Bureau of the Census 1997). However, approximately half of the recipients of public assistance have a disability. Curiously, government programs specifically earmarked for people with disabilities are determined and distributed according to how an ableist culture defines a disabled person. While Social Security Disability Insurance, special education services, and other entitlement programs are available, access to these services depends on how one is referred, evaluated, and labeled. Deaf performance artist Terry Galloway tells what happened when she needed new hearing aids during a personal economic slump:

> [M]y hearing aids, both of them, were busted, held together with masking tape. I had no choice. I had to go to the Rehabilitation Services and act deaf so I could get two government-issued hearing aids. So how do I act deaf? How do I convince these government officials that I am really deaf, which I really am, even if I don't look the part (although I don't even really know what it means to "look the part"). But the fate of my ears hinges on whatever performance of deafness that I come up with. (Beach and Pasternack 1998, 54)

Galloway, a vibrant physical performer, created a performance of deafness for the government officials that included a meek and glum demeanor with uncertain and blurry speech. "My perceived audience shaped my performance and they didn't even mean to," she mused (54). Whether intentional or not, dominant cultural assumptions about how a person with a disability should "perform" their impairment can limit access to basic needs.

To counter this constant construction of disability based on stereotypes, Wendell (1996) offers an alternate way to define disability based not solely on bodily function but on basic needs:

> Good definitions of impairment and disability should recognize that normal (i.e., unimpaired) physical structure and function, as well as normal (i.e., non-disabled) ability to perform activities, depend to some extent on the physical, social, and cultural environment in which a person is living, and are influenced by such factors as what activities are *necessary to survival* in an environment and what abilities a culture considers *most essential* to a participant. (22, emphasis mine)

This definition begins to situate ability in the same light as gender, race, and sexual orientation—not just as a biological phenomenon but also as part of complex social processes.

The Impact of Ableist Assumptions on Young People. As various multicultural theorists turn their attention to the increasing numbers of students labeled as "disabled," the focus is often placed on how teachers attempt to address "skills diversity" in today's classrooms (Heward and Cavanaugh 1997, 301). The most common disabilities facing young people are learning disabilities (50.5 percent), followed by speech or language impairment (23.4 percent), followed by mental retardation (12 percent) and serious emotional disturbance (8.5 percent) with other disabilities affecting 1 percent or less of children with disabilities (Beach Center on Families and Disability 1998). This diversity in abilities is generally expressed in terms of "exceptionality" in the context of school.

Curiously, Heward and Cavanaugh report that *exceptionality* refers to students with various disabilities *as well as* students who are gifted and talented (302). It would seem that a simplistic desire to avoid discrimination has resulted in the construction of a category that demands that these "special" students be excused from their regular classrooms for additional instruction. It is certainly common practice to supplement the needs of gifted and talented students and those students requiring extra assistance or additional work with help from specialized educational professionals.

Students who are suspected of being exceptional are referred, tested, labeled, and assigned additional instruction or professional help accordingly. While educational support services help provide equal access to the educational process for students with varying abilities, the politics of labeling are highly problematic within the context of the public schools in which a White middle-class set of assumptions are the yardstick against which behavior is measured. Many students are mislabeled because their "different" racial, ethnic, and class backgrounds do not match the expectations of teachers or administration. For example, Heward and Cavanaugh note that 26 percent of African American and 18 percent of Latina/o students are labeled with mild mental retardation while only 11 percent of White children are given this label (325). Moreover, research indicates that students are often reduced to their labels and performance expectations are lowered, which can result in a self-fulfilling prophecy of failure (Heward 1996).

Like the ADA legislation that protects the civil rights of people with disabilities, the Individuals with Disabilities Education Act (IDEA) protects a child's right to be educated in a public facility at no cost. Every child with a disability is entitled to an Individualized Education Program (IEP) that outlines appropriate goals for the student and a plan for implementation of those goals. Depending on the nature of a student's problems, the IDEA mandates that students with disabilities be educated in the least restrictive environment possible—preferably in a regular education classroom (Heward and Cavanaugh 314). As inclusion becomes more of a reality in classrooms and school districts across the country, finding positive ways to openly discuss and successfully accommodate a range of abilities is vital.

How Does Ability Affect Drama and Theatre Work? On the first day of a new series of drama classes, a young mother awkwardly approaches the registration table. It seems someone is hiding behind her coat, hindering her movement. She gives her registration form to the receptionist and after she has received all the paperwork she is introduced to the teacher for her child's section. "Now, where is Nikolas?" the teacher asks. A giggle emanates from underneath the coat. It's clear he is enjoying this game of shyness. "Can I say 'hello' to you, Nikolas?" the teacher asks, trying to coax him from his hiding place.

Nikolas finally emerges, a smile beaming across his severely disfigured six-year-old face—which catches the drama teacher off guard for a moment. "I wanna do drama!" he enthuses while his mother carefully studies the teacher's reaction. "Well," the teacher immediately responds, "you've come to the *right* place!"

A moment of "difference" has been catalogued and the journey toward inclusion begins. Young people with disabilities can often feel frustrated by a world that has difficulty accommodating them. How can drama teachers and theatre practitioners help provide a means for expression for all students and well as an environment that is respectful and accepting of a range of abilities? Knowing about how to approach some distinctive differences in ability may help.

Toward an Understanding of Different Abilities. A more comprehensive understanding of various physical and mental impairments can help alleviate the awkwardness many people with no known disabilities feel when confronted with the unfamiliar. Since ability is often not openly discussed, young people (and adults) have little knowledge about disabilities. They also often lack role models to provide examples of how to interact with people with disabilities or even how to begin discussing disabilities. The main areas of disability under consideration here include people who are hearing, visually, and mobility impaired, as well as people with cognitive disabilities. Here is a quick overview:

People who are Deaf or have a hearing impairment make up approximately 6.5 percent of the population in the United States (U.S. Bureau of the Census 1990). According to a recent document produced by the Kentucky Center for the Arts, the numbers of people who are Deaf or hard of hearing are increasing in the work force.[5] Contrary to popular belief, more people are hearing impaired rather than Deaf. Most have some residual hearing rather than none at all. The two main ways people who are Deaf or hearing impaired communicate are either through sign language or lip reading. American Sign Language (ASL) is not simply a translation of English but rather a language in its own right with its own grammar, syntax, and linguistic rules. ASL is much more effective than lip reading since many letters look the same. Extended conversations can be very difficult and exhausting. A default may be to try to write notes to the individual with a hearing impairment; however, not all people who are Deaf read and write.

People who are blind or visually impaired make up approximately 6 percent of the population (U.S. Bureau of the Census 1990). A person is considered legally blind if their vision is 20/200. Most people who are considered blind have some sight. Many people who are blind are very independent and mobile. While a large portion of those who are blind use Braille, many do not.

People who are mobility impaired make up approximately 3 percent of the population (U.S. Bureau of the Census 1990). There is a variety of reasons why an individual might use a wheelchair. Wheelchairs come in different sizes and shapes in order to meet an individual's needs especially since there is such a wide range of physical abilities among those who use them. Some people who use wheelchairs may also use canes, leg braces, or other assistive devices.

Of the people who are cognitively impaired, the largest percentage is composed of people with learning disabilities. Teachers in schools are most accustomed to dealing with this category, which includes, among other things, learning disabilities (LD), Attention Deficit Disorder (ADD), and Attention Deficit Hyperactive Disorder (ADHD). LD is an umbrella term for many different conditions that inhibit a person's ability to process and/or present information (Bailey 1993, 56). Because our ways of understanding involve our ability to take in sensory information, process it through the brain, and then use it in some way, the disconnect may occur in any of a number of places. Dyslexia, for example, involves a disconnect between visual information and its meaning. Letters are reversed, turned around, or actually moved. ADD and ADHD also involve a compromised ability to process sensory information.

Difficulty with focus and tendency towards distraction are key symptoms. ADHD adds a quality of "impulsiveness" to the mix.

Building Awareness

The lesson plans below use a variety of different drama techniques to address a range of issues concerning disability in age-appropriate ways. Younger elementary students consider how a physical disability can lead to discrimination. Older elementary students examine several negative assumptions about cognitive disabilities, such as dyslexia, as they create the story of young woman's struggle with school and learning.

TOPIC: ABILITY: PHYSICAL IMPAIRMENT

Focus How do assumptions about ability affect someone with a physical impairment?

Figure 6–1. Oliver's High Five *by Beverly Swerdlow Brown.*

Figure 6–2. *Oliver applies for an office job in* Oliver's High Five.

Teaching Objectives

To discuss stereotypes and preconceptions about ability and physical impairment;

To explore the issues and challenges that those stereotypes may cause;

To reflect on how we can work to change those stereotypes.

Target Age K–3rd grade

Time Needed Two 45-minute sessions

Materials

- An image of an octopus (such as a photograph, drawing, or toy).
- *Oliver's High Five* by Beverly Swerdlow Brown with illustrations by Margot J. Ott (Santa Fe, NM: Health Press, 1998). Oliver, an octopus who was born with five arms instead of eight, experiences discrimination as he tries to get a job.

Procedure

1. ENGAGE the students: Show the students an image of an octopus. Ask: *Who knows what this is? What do we know about where an octopus lives? What do they eat? Why do they need so many arms?* (Link to science information here as a way to expand on habitat issues as well as terminology—what "octo" means, etc.) *Today we are going to explore a story about an octopus who was born with five arms instead of eight. I wonder if he was treated any differently as a result. What do you think? Let's see what happened.*
2. SHARE the story: Gather students to read *Oliver's High Five.* In the story Oliver visits several possible places of employment. As you read, ask students how people treated him at each of the sites he visits. Ask how this might have made Oliver feel.
3. EXPLORE the story:
   a. Narrative statues: Ask students to stand up and find a space in the room. Narrate: *Imagine that you are Oliver. You have just decided to go and visit the human world. When I count to three, freeze in a position that shows how Oliver might be feeling about his adventure. Remember to use your whole body and face. One, two, three. Freeze, please.* Comment on their statues: *I see many statues that show how excited Oliver must be. Relax, please. Now, imagine that you are Oliver and you have just visited the pet store and the woman ran off in the back room and left you there. When I count to three, freeze in a position that shows how Oliver might be feeling. One, two, three. Freeze, please.* Comment on their statues: *I see a lot of statues that look confused, [other emotions]. Relax. Let's imagine that you are Oliver and you have just visited the hair salon and the woman told you that you cannot work there. How might Oliver be feeling? One, two, three. Freeze, please.* Comment. *Let's imagine that you are Oliver and you are talking to the woman at the gas station. How do you feel about her comment that you might scare customers away? One, two, three. Freeze, please.* Comment. *Let's imagine that you are Oliver and you're back at the pet store. The woman has just told you that you can have the job. How does that make you feel? One, two, three.* Comment. *Oliver went through so many different emotions in this story. Let's see if we can get a better idea about what caused all those emotions. I wonder what other people's actions have to do with how you feel about yourself?*
   b. Planning a story dramatization: Lead the group in brainstorming how they might bring Oliver's story to life: *Let's look more closely at how people's attitudes might have affected Oliver as he searched for a*

job at each of these places. If we were going to bring this story to life, what is the first thing that happened to Oliver that we might want to focus on? (List on a chalkboard, flip chart, or overhead.) Continue until you have an outline of possible scenes. Depending on time available and student skill level, you can choose to plan and play all of these scenes or ask students to pick one or two scenes they are most interested in finding out more about.
Possible scenes for this story include:

the beach

the pet store

the construction site

the hair salon

the office

the gas station

the pet store again

For each scene you play, ask students to list the characters needed to bring the scene to life. Consider what additional characters might be present (customers, other workers, etc.) in order to add more possibilities for including all students to take part in the scene. For example, if the group wants to start with Oliver's first visit to the pet store, possible characters include: the pet shop employee, Oliver, other customers, and various animals. Ask for volunteers to play each of these roles. You can use the whole class to enact this scene or just have half the class act at a time with the other half serving as "directors" and offering ideas for playing the material. (The two groups would switch roles in the playing of the next scene.)

Establish the setting for each scene by asking the students what the playing area should look like. For the pet store scene: *What can we use to suggest animal cages? How close together are the cages? Where is the door to the shop?*

c. Play the story: For each scene you choose to explore, ask the students to establish how the scene will begin and how it will end (either through narration provided by the leader or a line or an action performed by a character). Ask all the characters who will begin the scene to place themselves in the playing area. Play the scene improvisationally. Sidecoach as needed by providing narration or dialogue ideas.

d. Discuss: After each scene, ask the group to discuss how each incident affected Oliver: *How might Oliver have been able to be a good worker in this situation? How would you describe the pet store clerk's attitude toward Oliver? How might that make Oliver feel?* Repeat the previous step with other scenes as time and interest allow.

To strengthen drama skills, you can also evaluate and replay the scene by asking, *How clear was the scene? What might have been confusing? I noticed it was hard to hear Oliver because the animals were so loud. How could we make sure Oliver can be heard? and so on.*

e. Replay (optional): Depending on time and your focus for the work, replay each scene, incorporating the suggestions for making it stronger. Focus on how the replaying can help everyone better understand Oliver's dilemma.

4. REFLECT on the issues: *What kinds of attitudes about his abilities did Oliver encounter? Why do you suppose people have those kinds of attitudes? What changed the pet store worker's attitude about Oliver? What will it take to help change other people's attitudes about people with disabilities?*

5. EVALUATE the lesson: What did you notice about the group's willingness to discuss this issue? Was there any reluctance to engage? If so, why? What stereotypes were brought up? How do you feel you handled them? How did the students respond to the topic of disabilities and discrimination? What things still need to be examined? What questions did you have trouble answering? Which discussion segments worked best? Why? What do students seem most interested in concerning this issue? Based on your evaluation, how might you follow up this lesson?

Possible Extensions

Language Arts

Create a diary or sketch book that Oliver might have kept about his experiences in the human world.

Create a letter Oliver might have sent to his father about his new job.

Science

Link to information about undersea life and adaptation. How is Oliver's story an example of adaptation?

Health

Link to curriculum units on self-esteem. Create a poem or song about how to improve self-esteem.

TOPIC: ABILITY: COGNITIVE IMPAIRMENTS

Focus How do other people's attitudes about ability affect someone with a cognitive impairment?

Teaching Objectives

To discuss stereotypes and preconceptions about ability and cognitive impairment;

To explore the issues and challenges that those stereotypes may cause;

To relfect on how we can work to change those stereotypes.

Target Age 4th–6th grade

Time Needed Two or three 45-minute sessions

Materials

- *Thank You, Mr. Falker* by Patricia Polacco (New York: Philomel Books, 1998). Trisha has difficulty reading until a teacher helps her overcome her learning disability.
- Transparency with a lowercase *b* written as large as possible. (A poster board with the letters *p, q, b, d* could also work.)

Procedure

1. ENGAGE the students: Discuss what comes to mind when the students hear the word *stupid.* Ask why someone would call someone else "stupid." Ask what might make someone feel "stupid." Make a list of their comments. Discuss the fact that all students learn in different ways for many different reasons. *Sometimes when someone isn't as quick-witted as someone else or cannot read as well or as fast as someone else, they are labeled "stupid." For many, what is really going on is that their brain works in different ways than other people's brains. They might have a condition called a learning disability—meaning that they have difficulty making sense of things. There are many different kinds of learning disabilities. For example, take a look at this letter. It looks like an ordinary b doesn't it? But if you have dyslexia—a learning disability that affects the way your brain sees letters—you might see a d or p or even a q (or a 9 or 6) and get very confused and frustrated. And when you tried to read, the letters might look like they are swimming around and changing places while you try to sort out the words, and other people might call you "stupid." Even worse, you might think of yourself as "stupid." That's what happened to Trisha, a fifth-grade girl who was a fabulous artist but who was unable to read.*

2. SHARE the source material: Read or tell the story *Thank You, Mr. Falker,* in which a fifth grader named Trisha is frustrated about her ability to read. Analyze the illustrations by asking students specific questions, such as: *How might Trisha be feeling right now? What tells you that? What do you think is going through the teacher's mind? Let's try to get a better sense of her situation.*
3. EXPLORE the source material:
   a. Mirror work: Ask the group to imagine that you are someone like Trisha who is looking into a mirror. The students (as a group) will be your reflection in the mirror. Sit on a chair or stool in view of all class members and begin to enact a slow-motion scene about a young person who is frustrated by his or her attempts to read and write and who ends up drawing instead. Students are to "reflect" every movement you make. The scene might unfold as follows: Sit straight up and look around the room with nervous anticipation. See a book in front of you. Pick it up. Look around and slowly start to open it. Using your finger to follow the words, mime sounding out the words. Become more and more frustrated as the letters begin to "move around on the page." Rub your eyes or shake your head as you try to focus. Eventually slam the book down and cross your arms and pout. Next, look around the room, then pull out paper and a pencil. Look at it for a moment in awe, then begin to copy something off the board with large deliberate letters. Again, become confused as the letters seem to move and dance and do not make sense on the board or on the paper you are trying to write. Slam the pencil down, wad up the paper and throw it away, and hold your head in frustration. Next, pull out another piece of paper. Try to "secretly" keep it to yourself and begin to draw. Nod your head and smile as you look at your drawing. Quickly put it away and look up guiltily at an imaginary teacher.
   b. Discuss: Ask the students to identify what was happening in the story. *How did Trisha feel about reading? Writing? Drawing? What names might she be called by others in the class? What names might she call herself? Let's look at Trisha's story a little closer.*
   c. Image work: Ask for two volunteers to come to the front of the class. Ask one to be Trisha and have them stand straight and look ahead. Ask the other to be one of Trisha's classmates and to place their hands on their hips and look at Trisha. Muse about the possible meanings of this picture. *Now, suppose I told you that this is a story about some kind of "trouble at school." What's the story? What kind of relationship do these two have? I wonder what happened? I wonder*

what they might be thinking? I wonder what they might be saying? Discuss. *I wonder how those words might make Trisha feel about herself?*

Ask students to work in small groups of three or four to get a better sense of how other students treated Trisha. In each group, ask one student to play Trisha and the others to play classmates. Stress the ways in which people's bodies and facial expressions can communicate how they feel about something or someone. Encourage the student playing Trisha to show us how the other students' attitudes are affecting her. (Depending on time and drama experience, have students turn these into short scenes.)

Share these images. Discuss who the characters might be, what is going on, what the various characters might be getting ready to say, what Trisha might be thinking. Look for opportunities to ask who might be Trisha's ally in the class. *Do any of the students in the scenes seem to be supporting her? I wonder what it takes to be an ally and why it is sometimes so difficult to do?*

d. Role on the wall: Draw an outline of a body and ask: *What do we know so far about Trisha?* Write what is known on the outside of the body. Ask: *How might this character feel about the situation, themselves, others, and so on.* Write those comments on the inside of the body. Comment on how we don't always share or know about those inner feelings and explore together how those feelings can affect people and the decisions they make.

e. Scene work: In pairs, students create a scene between Trisha and one of her parents. Trisha's objective is to stay home from school to avoid feeling stupid. Her parent's objective is to get her to school so she can continue to learn. What happens? Have the pairs work simultaneously and occasionally ask everyone to freeze. "Spotlight" different groups by asking them to continue the scene for ten or twenty seconds while everyone gives them their attention. Freeze the spotlighted scene and ask the whole group to continue. Depending on time and experience with drama, have students show their scenes to the whole class one at a time. Add any new information you have discovered to Trisha's "role on the wall" outline. Brainstorm a list of questions students might want to have answered about what is going on inside Trisha's brain that makes her unable to read and write.

f. Teacher in role: Teacher takes on the role of a counselor who has come to talk to the teacher and the class. (Ask for a student volunteer to play the role of "teacher.") Start by telling the group that one of their class members is experiencing some difficulty and needs their help. Trisha has been absent frequently or going home sick often. Everyone knows that she's not really sick. The counselor asks what the situation is like in the classroom, what has been going on, asks the teacher to comment on what he or she thinks is going on. Reveal that testing has confirmed that Trisha has a cognitive disorder called dyslexia. Tell the class that you can begin to answer some questions they may have about it. Make a point to mention that incidents in which Trisha has been called "stupid" are far from true. She is very bright and talented. Her brain just has trouble giving her correct information about letters. Stress the need to be allies for one another to help aid in everyone's learning process. Out of role discuss what it means to be an ally. *Why are allies important? Who are your allies?*

g. Group statue: Mention that things changed for Trisha. Her teacher and a reading specialist helped her to break down the process of reading in a way that her brain could understand. After four months of intensive work, she was finally able to read. Many of her classmates also encouraged her in their own ways. Divide the class in half and ask the students to create a group statue says something about their success. Share the images. Discuss the fact that Trisha's success was connected to the whole class's success as a community of learners who learned a little more about what can happen when people are respectful of differences.

4. REFLECT on the issues: *What kinds of attitudes did Trisha encounter about her abilities at the beginning of this drama?* (Recall the initial images of interactions between Trisha and her classmates.) *Why do you suppose people have those kinds of attitudes? What began to change people's attitudes? What will it take to change attitudes about people with cognitive disabilities?*

5. EVALUATE the lesson: What did you notice about the group's willingness to discuss this issue? Was there any reluctance to engage? If so, why? What stereotypes were brought up? How do you feel you handled them? How did the students respond to the topic of disabilities and discrimination? What things still need to be examined? What questions did you have trouble answering? What discussion segments worked best? Why? What do students seem most interested in concerning this issue? Based on your evaluation, how might you follow up this lesson?

Possible Extensions

Language Arts

Create a scripted scene of the interactions that might have happened between Trisha and her classmates *before* they became her allies.

Create a scripted scene of the interactions that might have happened between Trisha and her classmates *after* they became her allies.

Social Studies

Discuss how the term *ally* applies to encounters between governments and nations.

Art

Create a drawing or painting that expresses Trisha's frustrations about her reading ability.

Create a drawing or painting that expresses Trisha's feelings after she begins to get help.

Science

Look at how the brain functions and how different parts of the brain affect different perceptual abilities.

Creating an Environment for Equity

With an increased awareness of "ableist" assumptions, our everyday actions can reflect an open and respectful attitude toward ability. Your mindfulness can also invite your students and patrons to rethink their assumptions and attitudes. By modeling an openness and accommodation for a range of abilities, students occupying a variety of positions on the ability spectrum might participate more freely in drama and theatre work. Below are several suggestions for considering language use, planning, and student support as you explore diversity and ability.

Language. Model and encourage "people first" language—such as "people with disabilities" rather than "the disabled" or "the handicapped." As Access Austin Arts asserts, "disabilities don't handicap—attitudes and architecture do."[6] They suggest focusing on the person and not on the disability. For example, develop the habit of saying things like "people who are deaf" or "a person who is hearing impaired" instead of a "deaf person"; "people who use wheelchairs" or "with mobility impairments" instead of "confined to a wheelchair" or "wheelchair bound"; "an individual with a physical disability" instead of "crippled" or "handicapped"; "an individual with multiple disabilities," instead of "deformed" or "a freak"; "a person who has a mental illness," instead of "crazy" or "nuts"; "an individual with a developmental disability" instead of a "retard" or a "moron."

The National Endowment for the Arts (1994) reiterates that attention to language is important. Terminology such as "afflicted by MS" or "AIDS victim" tends to emotionalize and sensationalize a person's disability. Referring to people with disabilities as "courageous" or "heroic" implies that the person is a hero or a martyr. Referring to people without any known disabilities as "normal" implies that people with disabilities are somehow abnormal.

Related terms or phrases in popular culture should be examined for their connotations. "That's so lame," is a common expression but is as offensive an expression as other offensive racist and sexist epithets. Would you use the expression if someone with a physical impairment was in the room?

Planning. Any discussion of ability is tied to considerations about learning styles. Work to make all assignments and the regular operation of your class as accessible as possible to your visual, verbal, and kinesthetic learners. Occasionally point out why you use these various strategies as a way to help demystify the notion of multiple learning styles.

Diane Nutting (1999), formerly with the National Theatre of the Deaf, suggests that teachers plan carefully how they will use their classroom space to make sure that the environment is accessible. Consider how you can set up the space to best facilitate the learning processes for all your students. Anticipate challenges that the space might present for your diverse learners. If you aren't sure about how the environment might be difficult for students, just ask them.

When planning work to accommodate a broad spectrum of student abilities, Rachel Briley (1999), a professor at Western Michigan State University, suggests that teachers should begin by closely examining the goals of any activity you are planning to use with students. If, for example, you are planning to do a choral reading exercise and you have a student who is deaf in the class, you may be worried about how you might be able to include him in the exercise. By considering your goals for the exercise and what the "essence of the experience" is, Briley believes that you will be able to adapt the activity to accommodate the abilities of a variety of students. At the core of a choral reading exercise is a chance to explore sound and how sound can express emotion. This often happens through duration, quality, tone, and pitch, which can communicate a state of being, a feeling, an action, or a motivation. Instead of asking the student who is deaf to participate vocally, which would be an unnatural and meaningless activity, consider how you might make available other ways of exploring those same qualities of sound through movement, light, or color. Any of those tangible and visual elements would capture the essence of the experience without excluding the student from making discoveries.

Student supports. For working in a mixed ability or inclusion class (any classroom, really!), Mary Pearce's 1996 article on "Inclusion: Twelve Secrets to Making it Work" provides several ideas gleaned from their interviews with master teachers:

1. Develop classroom rules that have consistent consequences. Respecting others and keeping safe are the basics. One teacher reports that she asks her students to brainstorm and then post what the rules should look like and sound like so students can keep themselves honest.
2. Focus on structure. Often students with disabilities or special needs succeed best in environments with a routine and clear ideas about what is expected. One teacher reported having photographs that illustrate what a neat desk looks like. A photo of students in a circle or of a group working well together might be useful for drama practitioners. A visual template of the steps in decision making has been useful in role-playing situations in the past.
3. Ask for help when you need it from special education teachers, school counselors, or other professionals who may know more about a particular disability than you do.
4. Be clear about how you expect your students to act, treat, and talk to and about students with disabilities. One teacher reports that she talks to her students openly about students with special needs and says that they may require special assignments or ways of working in the classroom that could benefit all students. Talk openly about every student's needs and goals.
5. Working in mixed cooperative groups can put students in peer mentoring and tutoring situations that will help them thrive.

Above all, strive to create an environment that enables students to safely discuss disability-related issues and to treat each other with mutual respect.

Questions to Ponder

1. Consider your own abilities and areas of impairment. How would you situate yourself in relationship to ability? When did you first become aware of ability as an issue? When did you first become aware of impairments and their impact? What incidents or situations brought up this awareness?

2. How would you describe the abilities of the students you ordinarily work with? What tensions does "skills diversity" bring to your ability to work together? How might your assumptions about ability affect your work with these students? What might you do to eliminate any bias or possibility for discrimination?
3. How would you categorize the "skills diversity" of your peers in your working environment? What would you say is the role of ableism in your group? How do the ability levels and attitudes of your various colleagues affect relationships between peers?
4. The controversy over referring, evaluating, and labeling African American and Latina/o students as either mildly mentally retarded or learning disabled is raging in many schools. Some say this practice is no different from the "racial profiling" techniques that police officers use as an excuse for stopping Black and Latina/os for traffic violations. What do you think? Is that just a simple case of racism that classifies race as a disability or is something else going on here?
5. There is great debate over how students who have been labeled as having disabilities should be educated. Should they spend most of their time in the "least restrictive environment" possible (meaning a regular education classroom), be assigned to full-time special classes in public schools, or be assigned to special schools with either day or residential options? What do you think? Why? Which environment is most likely to give students the greatest opportunity to succeed in both the long and short term? Why? What other options are there?

Practical Problems to Consider

1. Working with a retelling of Rumpelstiltskin as a source for creative drama or theatre work, how would you structure the work so the issue of disability can be explored?
2. You are working with a mixed-race group of mixed-ability fourth graders. As they are to embark on small group work, the members of one group come up to you and complain bitterly about a Black student they have been assigned to work with. He has ADHD and is alternately hyperactive and unfocused. How do you respond?
3. When working for the first time with a mixed-race group of multiaged students in an afterschool program, a teacher comes up and pats you on the back sympathetically. "I can't believe you got stuck with this group," she sighs. "It's like your own private special ed class! Good luck!" How do you respond? How might you plan differently after having this information?

4. A third-grade colleague wants to tackle the issue of disabilities with his students and wants your advice. He is thinking about having students do a Blind Walk and a few sensory isolation exercises (touch, hearing, sight) so students can "see what it's like to be blind, deaf, and handicapped." How might you help him create a compelling lesson that introduces "people first" language, among other things?
5. You realize that many areas in your working environment (school, community center, theatre, or other location) are not accessible to many students with disabilities. Although you are not quite sure what the ADA code requires, you know something needs to be done. However, when you bring this up with your colleagues there is a great deal of opposition to even exploring what could be done. Cost is cited as a predominant issue. There are just too many other resource demands on your organization. How do you respond? What action is needed to explore this issue further? Read the stipulations outlined in the ADA code. What are the legal ramifications of not complying? What do you do next?

A Case Study Situation

Your class or theatre group has been asked to create a performance about "disability and diversity" as part of a series of diversity awareness activities your organization is sponsoring. One of the goals of these activities is to address the civil rights issues associated with disability. One member of your group jokes that this is will be a little hard to work on because none of you has any disabilities. In fact, no one has any visible disabilities but at least 20 percent of your group has an impairment of some kind that is never discussed openly. How do you approach the subject with the group? Think about a possible scenario for your performance that centers on tension over disability rights. How do you represent disability in your performance? How do you avoid easy stereotypes in favor of complex and interesting characters? How does the group's own experience of various levels of disability feed into the work?

Resources for Drama and Theatre Work on Disability

Picture Books

Be Good to Eddie Lee by Virginia Fleming (New York: Putnam, 1993). A girl reluctantly befriends a boy with Down's syndrome and discovers the uniqueness of his perspective on life.

Dina the Deaf Dinosaur by Carole Addabbo (Stamford, CT: Hannacroix Creek Books, 1998). A Deaf dinosaur runs away from home after a dispute with her parents about sign language.

Friends at School by Rochelle Bunnett (New York: Star Bright Books, 1995). Pictures and stories of how a mixed-ability group of young children works and plays together at school.

Seeing in Special Ways: Children Living with Blindness by Thomas Bergman (Milwaukee, WI: Gareth Stevens Children's Books, 1989). Children with visual impairments are interviewed about how they use their other senses to help them "see." Includes many photographs.

The Secret Code by Dana Meachen Rau (New York: Children's Press, 1998). A boy who is visually impaired teaches a friend how to read Braille.

Plays

Hush: An Interview with America by James Still. In Hush, Kansas, a twelve-year-old with a visual impairment becomes the talk of the nation in this play about growing up, inner vision, and personal voice. (Available from Dramatic Publishing: 203-254-6624 or e-mail: <dramaticpb@aol.com>.)

General Resources on Disability

Bailey, S. D. 1993. *Wings to Fly: Bringing Theatre Arts to Students with Special Needs.* Rockville, MD: Woodbine House. An excellent resource for doing drama and theatre in special education settings. Lots of solid practical information.

Davis, L, ed. 1997. *The Disability Studies Reader.* New York: Routledge. The first collection of scholarship in the emerging field of disability studies. Useful for those who want delve into how disability is currently being theorized from a variety of points of view.

Kempe, A., ed. 1996. *Drama Education and Special Needs.* Cheltenham, U.K.: Stanley Thornes. This edited volume brings together the practical experiences of several drama practitioners in the U.K. who work with young people with a range of special needs.

Peter, M. 1995. *Making Drama Special: Developing Drama Practice to Meet Special Educational Needs.* London: David Fulton. Focuses on the nuts and bolts of planning and implementing reflective drama practice with children who have special needs.

Wendell, S. 1996. *The Rejected Body: Feminist Philosophical Reflections on Disability.* New York: Routledge. A provocative view of what it means to be "disabled" from a feminist point of view. Elegantly written and clearly argued.

Notes

1. I am using the convention proposed by James Woodward (1972) in my capitalization of the term *Deaf* to refer to individuals who self-identify as part of a particular cultural group with a shared language (American Sign Language). Lowercase *deaf* refers to the clinical condition of not hearing.

2. This is a term Gene Mirus shared with me in a recent e-mail correspondence (1999).

3. I am borrowing Leonard Davis's use of the term "temporarily abled" from his book *Enforcing Normalcy* (1995, 172). He uses this term to make specific commentary on fact that there are no "normal" people. Further, the term *normal* reinforces the normal/disabled binary.

4. See Davis 1995 (Chapter 7) for a more complete discussion of this point.

5. From the Kentucky Center for the Arts, "Guide to Etiquette and Behavior for Working with Persons with Disabilities." In this section I have paraphrased several key comments from this useful document. For more information about their accessibility programming, contact Alice Baldwin at 502-562-0111.

6. I am grateful to Access Austin Arts for the information in this section. For further information, contact them at 512-454-9912 or by fax at 512-451-3110. For a look at their complete guidelines and information about accessibility, see their website at <http://www.main.org/accessarts/people1st.htm.>

Postscript: "Looking on . . ."

Bringing theory and practice together is not always easy. In the previous chapters, I have attempted to illustrate how various theories of identity formation and "locatedness" have affected the ways in which I structure my work and "act" as an artist and teacher. It is often much simpler to just "do the work" than to reflexively analyze the assumptions guiding our practice. The tendency to privilege "doing" over "thinking about what is done" points to how unsettling it can be to question your practice. Similarly, the introduction of new ways of looking at the work can be disconcerting. How can various theoretical lenses help us connect "thinking" and "doing" and move us closer to an embodied practice of pluralism in drama and theatre work?

In her book, *Bitter Milk*, educational theorist Madeline Grummet (1988) points out that the word theory has religious origins:

> The *theoros* was a representative sent from his Greek city to observe sacred festivals in other cities. Through *theoria*, "looking on," he abandoned himself to those events, to their version of the cosmic order, and strove to imitate its ordered relationships and proportions in his own self-formation. (184)

Envisioning theory as a way of "looking on" and closely observe how things are ordered and connected to self-formation can be a very useful metaphor for drama teachers and practitioners. Lakoff and Johnson (1980) tell us that metaphor "is pervasive in everyday life, not just in language but in thought and action" (3). They point out that, in Western culture, the search for a more concrete way to express the process of ideation results in a focus on light and visuality—"understanding is seeing; ideas are light sources, discourse is a light medium" (48). Consider our language related to "knowing": "I see what you're saying." "I view it differently." "Now I've got the whole picture."

I evoke this metaphor of visuality and light as a way to consider how "looking on" through various theoretical lenses might usefully inform our practice. When theory, in the broadest sense of the word, is self-consciously applied, it can provide a way to "illuminate," even if for only a fleeting moment, and help us question "the order of things" in our field. As a tool for illumination, theory can challenge and improve our practice by attuning our ability to "see" the impact of our work more clearly.

Some practitioners may feel that "theory" has nothing to do with theatre and drama work. As I have argued elsewhere, however, we cannot escape theory. There is a theory or particular way of seeing the world implicit in even our most commonplace sets of assumptions. The various critical theories considered in previous chapters can help us be more reflexive about what we see and do. This self-conscious use of theory helps us to intentionally place our attention and bring assumptions to the foreground instead of keeping them hidden.

What differentiates a critical theory from a commonplace set of assumptions is the degree of reflexivity involved. Resistance to theory (or "looking on"), as Terry Eagleton (1983) points out, generally indicates a resistance to *somebody else's* theory while at the same time obscuring your own (viii). Theory and theorizing "happens" whether we are paying attention or not. Even if we wish to remain outside theory and therefore innocent of the implications of examining our commonplace assumptions, we cannot. Instead of denying the challenge of "looking on," my argument throughout this book has been concerned with the act of responsibly accounting for the theoretical underpinnings and assumptions that, consciously or unconsciously, inform our work and our self-formations.

The questions raised in this book are part of a larger conversation about diversity in our field. As teachers and practitioners, let's examine the implications of difference, pluralism, and diversity in each of our own contexts. Please add your voice to this dialogue. Theorizing "difference" can help us "look on" and see more clearly the detailed gradations of light and the interplay of shadows. It can also challenge us to expand and enlarge our thinking, our practice, and our research. Let's not back away. We are only just learning the rules of engagement. How we deal with the resultant ambiguity and complexity remains to be seen.

Appendix: Some Drama Basics

As a drama practitioner, I use a wide range of drama and theatre techniques. And like most educators and practitioners, the type of practice I choose at any given moment is directly linked to context and purpose. The purpose of this book is twofold: 1) to explore how drama and theatre work can be used as a tool for discussion, exploration, and reflection about diversity; 2) to clarify how teachers and practitioners can be sensitive to diversity issues in their drama and theatre practice. Although a good deal of what follows is directed at improvisational classroom drama work, many of the underlying goals, pedagogical concerns, planning tips, activities, and management techniques can also be useful for creating devised or scripted theatre work.

Underlying Notions

In *Beginning Drama 4–11,* Joe Winston and Miles Tandy (1998) offer an excellent overview of several principles underlying drama practice:

1. Drama is playful.
2. Dramas use stories to explore issues of human significance.
3. In drama, the normal rules of time, place, and identity are suspended.
4. Drama is a social activity and a communal art form.
5. Drama is driven by rules and conventions.
6. Drama should not be boring. (x)

To elaborate, drama is playful activity that immediately engages precisely because of its playful nature. With roots in dramatic pretend play, fictional stories about people "in a mess" (as British drama practictioner Dorothy Heathcote has often been quoted as saying) are at the heart of any drama experience. In classroom drama, participants explore the range of human dilemmas and foibles—from the absurdly comedic to the deadly serious, and all points between. When we work in drama, we are able to suspend ordinary physics to negotiate time and place as well as identity. We also have the added benefit of critically examining how this fictional "time out" resonates with our ordinary experience of the world and with what we think and believe. We embark on this journey with others and, as a result, have the opportunity to strengthen our ability to relate as well as to create together. Social encounters are necessarily governed by rules, as are artistic endeavors. Successful creation requires carefully negotiated boundaries. The late drama practitioner Barbara Wills often encouraged her pre-service teachers to "limit to free"—reinforcing the connection between clear guidelines and the creative process. Obviously, our work loses its impact if it becomes boring. By using engaging subject matter, varying activities, attending to the rhythm of a lesson, and strategically using tension, contrast, and surprise we sustain student engagement—not to mention our own.

Pedagogically Speaking

My particular style and approach to drama as illustrated in the lesson plans included in this book is an eclectic blending of the wisdom, talents, and discoveries of many other practitioners. My pliant methodology is further complicated as dramatic approaches and activities are interpreted through various critical lenses. As I outlined in the preface, my practice has benefited enormously from constructivist understandings of learning (i.e., each person constructs knowledge of themselves; teachers and artists create environments in which this can occur). Context sensitivity and the strategic use of critical thinking skills further complicate this theorizing. In addition, feminist theory and pedagogy brings questions about truth and identity formation to the work.

Broadly speaking, my overall goals for the lesson plans included in this book are to give students an opportunity to think critically together and to construct their own understandings of diversity as they also strengthen their drama skills. Along the way they have the opportunity to openly explore and evaluate how people behave toward one another and to imagine and rehearse different options. Instead of me as a teacher telling them what to do, how to think, or how to act, students make the discoveries themselves through a combination of dramatic action and critical reflection. Is it hard? Yes. Is it frustrating? Sometimes. Patience and openness is vital if you believe in giving students the space and time they need to make discoveries through drama (a lesson I am still struggling to learn).

How do we avoid "teacher-pleasing" behavior in this kind of work? Students are often very savvy about sorting out "what teachers want." If a practitioner is committed to creating opportunities in which *students* make decisions, construct their own knowledge, *and* critique their constructions rather than "give" them the preferred answers (either overtly or covertly), students will (more often than not) direct their attention toward the work rather than simply aping what the teacher wants to hear. We can never escape the power dynamics inherent in the classroom situations—nor should we. We need to be aware, however, of the power of the tacit approval that often resides in the teacher (or other power figures). This can be ameliorated *if* the teacher or artist is comfortable enough with themselves and clear enough about their pedagogical motives to redirect that power into the students' learning experiences.

Lesson Planning

I define a lesson plan as a structured learning opportunity that unfolds over time. It may be expanded or contracted due to a variety of reasons, including student interest or needs, teacher comfort, curricular connections, and so on. The majority of the lesson plans in this volume are not meant to be contained in one instructional session. I have indicated an approximate optimal time frame for each plan, although any of these lessons can be expanded or contracted for specific needs and contexts.

You will notice that the lesson plans included here are very complete. This is partially due to consistent feedback from elementary teachers and practitioners indicating a preference for detailed lesson plans as models for future planning. None of these plans is intended to be used verbatim. Instead they are examples of how I teach—what I do, what I tend to say, and how I ask questions. Your style and preoccupations will be different. Please employ them to the degree that they are useful for you—but I expect you will want to adapt, morph, and select according to your own comfort level and interests. These lesson plans are probably most useful as examples of ways to structure for critical thinking and reflection about sensitive issues.

Each lesson plan unfolds through a carefully considered structure. At the outset I am careful to note the topic as well as the focus of each lesson. I have found it useful to frame the focus as a question that motivates the lesson. I have also included specific teaching objectives to help guide the lesson structure and desired outcomes. I divide the body of each lesson into the following components:

1. Engaging the students: I try to strategically plan for ways to "hook" the students and create an atmosphere of curiosity in the opening moments of any lesson.
2. Sharing the story or source material: All the lesson plans included here are built around interesting and compelling stories or source materials following what Cecily O'Neill (1995) calls a "pretext" for the drama work. I have generally started with storybooks as a touchstone, although I use them selectively. Sometimes I read or tell all or part of the narrative situation depending on my objectives. I often stress the implications of narrative dilemma rather than the actual storyline.
3. Exploring the story: Depending on my focus and objectives I use a variety of activities to explore the story or source material as outlined below.
4. Reflecting on the issues with the students: This is a crucial step that can occur at the end of a lesson or at several key points within a lesson. As indicated in the activities listed below, reflection can take many forms—from discussion to writing to various kinds of active strategies.
5. Evaluating the lesson as a teacher: I believe we each become stronger as educators and artists by critically evaluating our work. At the end of each lesson I pose several challenging questions for the leader to consider. As a reflective practitioner, how do you make sense of what happened in this lesson?

As I plan a lesson I also take into consideration the age appropriateness of the activities I am choosing. For younger students, I often include more physical activities such as narrative pantomime work along with a good deal of simultaneous playing and acting out stories together. At the older elementary level, simultaneous work is supplemented by small- and large-group role-playing along with more carefully composed image work and in-depth process drama.

I have intentionally left specific student objectives out of these lesson plans. Since these plans are designed to explore particular subject matter in more depth, my focus for these lessons is on structuring opportunities for young people to think more critically about the assumptions that lie behind each of these identity locations. This is not to say that I only use drama for subject exploration without regard to curricular or social skill development. A classroom teacher or theatre arts specialist at the elementary level could easily tailor and reshape these plans to include student objectives that have to do with drama (such as character development, ensemble skills, improvisation in a group) or with other curricular topics (persuasion skills, weighing evidence, fictional narrative writing, mapping skills) which would add an extra layer of questions to the suggested evaluation points.

Lastly, I have attempted to avoid opportunities for students to rehearse or reinforce stereotypes within these lesson plans. For example, a choice to have students create a frozen image of a "family" at the outset of the lesson on *Asha's Mums* could result in reinforcing stereotypical nuclear family scenes. Pedagogically, I want to avoid setting up work and then saying "Now, what's wrong with this?" Waiting until after the lesson to have students depict a variety of families might net more interesting results and give them the opportunity to apply their new discoveries about different kinds of families. Certainly a case can be made for critically engaging students in a discussion about why, for example, an exclusive focus on portraying nuclear families might be symptomatic of the normative assumptions we receive about families. However, at the moment I am interested in constructing new images and concepts instead of merely deconstructing old ones. We cannot prove or deny that reproducing stereotypes reinforces them, even if our intention is to break them down. That being the case, I try to avoid rehearsing stereotypes as much as I can. Am I completely successful? No, but part of the "embodied practice" of diversity is being vigilant about what you put out there.

Role of the Artist/teacher

A drama teacher or practitioner occupies a unique position. They can alternately be a catalyst for engaging interest and making connections; a facilitator of creative work, discussion, and the thinking process; and a servant subordinate to the students' needs and well-being.

Unique to this role are a host of specific skills, including how to: manage a group, get consensus, establish boundaries, deal with behavior issues, give directions, ask questions, listen, muse, share decision making, strategize, know when to make it hard (add pressure and tension) and when to ease up during dramatic moments and during reflection and critical evaluation. I have attempted to give examples of how these teaching strategies might work in context of the ten lesson plans in this book.

Questioning is one of the most important drama tools for a practitioner interested in developing critical awareness. Juliana Saxton and Norah Morgan (1987) outline a taxonomy of questioning based on a revisioning of Benjamin Bloom's taxonomy of educational objectives. Their framework encourages practitioners to consider how to structure questions (and I would add lesson plans) that ask students to recall, clarify, apply, analyze, synthesize, and judge to take full advantage of how our work can connect the processes of "doing" and "thinking."

Activities for Drama

For the drama work under consideration in this text, I have divided the overview of activities into the following categories:

1. Activities for engagement and skill-building
2. Activities for exploring and scene-building
3. Activities for analyzing and reflecting

I tend to organize my drama activities according to Ruth Heinig's suggestions: 1) as solo pantomime work, 2) as paired or group pantomime work, 3) as solo verbal work, or 4) as paired or group verbal work (1992: 7). Group work can be pursued in small groups or as a large group depending on context and content. Structuring various activities in and around a central story or source material in a way that accounts for rhythm and progression is part of the artistry of teaching.

Activities for Engagement and Skill-building

As is obvious in most of the lesson plans, I tend to start with something that will immediately engage students. Often I use an object or visual stimulus, a question, or an activity. Many games can serve this purpose while at the same time "exercising" the skills and tools the students will use in drama, such as voice, body, and imagination. Games can also serve an important metaphoric function. For example, the mirror activity used in the lesson on cognitive impairments in Chapter 6 can serve as a metaphor for what it takes to work together as an ensemble, or for the art of careful observation, or imitation, or plagiarism. Discoveries about problem-solving, metaphoric connections, and links to other subject matter become more apparent as the teacher leads discussions after or between cycles of these activities.

I often use simple pantomime activities to initially engage students in a topic or theme. Count and Freeze pantomime work, inspired by Ruth Heinig, is basic activity that involves individuals or groups pantomiming a situation while the leader counts from one to five (or ten) and then says "Freeze." Depending on the context, you may want the pantomimer(s) to start in a frozen position as well. This can be a guessing activity focusing on skill development or as a way to explore a concept more fully in a controlled manner. Likewise statue work can provide an excellent "way in" to a drama session.

Activities for Exploring and Scene-building

After source material has been shared and initially examined, it can be explored in a variety of ways, using some of the techniques below. I often begin an examination of character or motivation through various Narrative Pantomime techniques (also inspired by Ruth Heinig). This simultaneous pantomime activity involves a situation or story that is narrated by the leader. Students enact a moment in the life of a central "protagonist" or alternately a series of characters. The narration should contain little or no dialogue and be full of colorful action, sensory experiences, or exploration of feelings or emotions. It is useful to shape the improvised or prepared narration in a second-person format: "You reach up and pick the reddest apple on the tree," etc.

Exercises such as Vote with Your Feet (which is used in the lesson plan on gender equity) help assess student knowledge, received understandings, and current opinions about the topic under consideration. By reading statements and asking them to gather in designated areas according to whether they agree, disagree, or aren't sure, teachers can immediately open up speculation on how beliefs are shaped and help develop dramatic material that is relevant to the participants.

I also rely heavily on various kinds of image work (inspired by Augusto Boal's image theatre) as a key way to begin exploring topics. Also known as Frozen Pictures, Freeze Frame, or Cartooning, this exercise asks students to create concrete pictures or abstract visual representations of situations or concepts with their bodies. Processing this work through careful questioning is key to developing a critical eye as we move through the drama experience.

Following the work of Dorothy Heathcote and Cecily O'Neill, I often use "teacher in role" as a strategy to explore the implications of the source material. I find it gives me a way to "turn up the heat," challenge and provoke while at the same time giving students a great deal of say in how things should proceed. I also use a "mantle of the expert" approach that asks students to think like various professionals as a way to gain different perspectives on the situation at hand.

For further exploration, I generally progress to scene-oriented work that is often "framed" in different ways: video clips, news broadcasts, flashbacks, dreams, surveillance camera footage, etc. Depending on the experience of a group, I also use a version of Boal's forum theatre work by asking students to share their scene a second time and have the "audience" look for moments in which the protagonist could have made a different choice to achieve a desired outcome. Anyone with a different solution is encouraged to replace the protagonist and try their idea. After the intervention, the class evaluates the effectiveness of the solution. This can lead to excellent discussions and critical analysis.

Activities for Analyzing and Reflecting

There are several strategies for analyzing and reflecting on drama work. Following Morgan and Saxton's taxonomy, discussions and drama work can be structured to culminate in higher-order thinking skills such as analyzing, judging, and applying new knowledge. For me, this is a crucial step in the process of doing drama.

Scene work designed to examine a situation that has been under investigation as an "object"—such as the news report on the custody trial outlined in Chapter 5—can serve as a dramatic way to analyze the subject matter. Similarly, drama-related writing (such as letters to the editor) and drawing (the most significant moment in the drama, for example) can provide a way to reflect on relevant issues. Image work can also provide a way to mark the important moments while "hotseating" a central character can offer students the opportunity to give a final piece of advice or summarize a situation from a particular point of view.

Many elementary teachers already use journaling to enhance writing skills. Drama gives students something concrete to write about. Designated drama journals can also be used as a way to encourage students to reflect on their drama-based experiences. I often use drama journals as a place for students to record their thoughts and reactions that they may not have been able to express during our lesson. I also encourage students to express themselves in their in journals in whatever medium is best suited for them—including drawing and collage.

Other Considerations: Establishing Rules and Getting Attention

Drama work can induce a high degree of engagement that can sometimes lead to a level of noise and chaos that can scare off beginners (and their administrators!). "Drama rules" provide boundaries within which young people can safely create. Most drama rules help establish how students treat one another and, as needed, how they treat their teachers. Rules will depend on the age and experience of the participants—and the personality and tolerance of the teachers. Rules go hand in hand with consequences. Be very clear and consistent about your expectations and the consequences of choosing *not* to follow the agreed-upon rules. Let students know if you will use a "warning" system. Giving one warning and then asking a child to sit out until they feel they can cooperate with others sends a clear message about rules and consequences. There is no reason to be angry with a child who chooses to ignore the rules, but rather express your disappointment that she or he *made a choice* not to participate for the moment. Look for ways to praise students for making choices that reinforce the agreed-upon drama rules and enhance the group's ability to work together. Possible rules include:

Respect self and others at all times.

Listen to whoever is speaking.

Cooperate and concentrate.

No touching during role-playing.

One of my favorite tactics is to ask students what rules *they* think the group needs in order to do drama together effectively and to establish their own consequences. Finally, look for positive ways to help students understand their boundaries by clearly delineating the perimeters of your drama space and which objects they can work with, and by modeling positive ways in which they can interact.

Sample Devices for Getting Attention

Even if you establish clear boundaries and rules, classroom management during drama work can present a unique challenge for the teacher. Specific management techniques are usually needed when a teacher needs the students' attention and/or focus in order to continue on to the next phase of the work. Consider the following:

- Musical instruments such as a tambourine or a triangle can be a good way to signal young children that you need everyone to gather around you or to give you their attention. Practice a few times so children get used to the device.
- Turn off the lights and/or quickly flip them on and off as a signal for students to quiet down.
- Establish the word *freeze* as a way to get students to stop what they are doing and pay attention.
- Announce softly: "Clap once if you can hear the sound of my voice." Wait for a few students to clap. "Clap twice if you can hear the sound of my voice," and so on, until you have everyone's attention.

- Your silence can also be very effective. Creative drama pioneer Winifred Ward used to sit quietly and look at the floor until everyone noticed her and quieted down.
- Announce that students should gather as quickly as possible in a designated place (such as a corner) in a designated way (such as in a circle) by the time you count to five (or ten, or another number).
- Establish a call-and-response mechanism. For example, when the teacher says, "Focus," students are to respond by saying, "Check." This can work with a variety of word pairs or phrases. Also, clapping out a rhythm that the students must imitate can be a great signal for attention.

Whatever you do, avoid yelling over the noise! Establish a device or two and use them consistently. Change tactics if a device becomes ineffective or overly familiar. Above all, find a way to enjoy the creative chaos that doing drama entails!

Ten Good Resources for Beginners

Fleming, M. 1998. *Starting Drama Teaching.* London: David Fulton. Good, practical introduction to what it takes to teach drama.

Heinig, R. 1992. *Improvisation with Favorite Tales.* Portsmouth, NH: Heinemann. Concise practical ideas for creating drama lessons around folk tales.

Neelands, J. 1991. *Structuring Drama Work.* Cambridge, U.K.: Cambriidge University Press. An invaluable "recipe book" of techniques for drama work as well as useful information on structuring lessons.

O'Neill, C. and A. Lambert. 1982. *Drama Structures.* London: Hutchinson. An excellent overview of the theory and practice of process drama along with annotated lesson structures that model how teachers can plan in response to student input.

Saldaña, J. 1995. *Drama of Color: Improvisation with Multiethnic Folklore.* Portsmouth, NH: Heinemann. Terrific collection of lesson plans structured around ethnically diverse folktales.

Spolin, V. 1983. *Improvisation for the Theatre.* Evanston, IL: Northwestern University Press. Essential handbook of improvisational activities for skill-building and theatrical exploration.

Tarlington, C. and W. Michaels. 1995. *Building Plays.* Markham, Ontario: Pembroke. A step-by-step guide for creating performance events from process-oriented drama work.

Tarlington, C. and P. Verriour. 1991. *Role Drama.* Portsmouth, NH: Heinemann. A useful beginner's guide to how role drama can be effective in the classroom. Excellent overview of how to plan a role drama.

Warren, Kathleen. 1994. *Hooked on Drama.* Waverly, New South Wales: Macquarie University, Institute of Early Childhood. Provides excellent information on doing process-oriented drama techniques with young children. The clear and elegant statement of philosophy is useful for any drama practitioner.

Winston, J. and M. Tandy. 1998. *Beginning Drama 4–11.* London: David Fulton. Good step-by-step introduction to drama work through an in-depth examination of a lesson, along with several ideas for using drama across the curriculum. Nice section on progression and assessment.

Five Good Resources for Advanced Work

Boal, Augusto. 1992. *Games for Actors and Non-actors.* New York: Routledge. An excellent source for unique games and in-depth explanation of image and forum theatre work.

Heathcote, D. and G. Bolton. 1995. *Drama for Learning.* Portsmouth, NH: Heinemann. A comprehensive look at the "mantle of the expert" approach developed by Dorothy Heathcote.

Morgan, N. and J. Saxton. 1987. *Teaching Drama: A Mind of Many Wonders.* London: Hutchinson. Examines the skills needed to be an effective drama leader. Full of practical advice and exercises to help specialists hone their craft.

O'Neill, C. 1995. *Drama Worlds: A Framework for Process Drama.* Portsmouth, NH: Heinemann. An in-depth analysis of process drama and ways to enhance the experience of drama.

Woolland, B. 1993. *The Teaching of Drama in the Primary School.* London: Longman. Excellent practical information about using drama across the curriculum as well as moving from improvisation into production.

Works Cited

Access Austin Arts. 1999. "People First Language at All Times!" *Access Austin Arts Home Page.* 20 September. <http://www.main.org/accessarts/people1st.htm>.

Adams, M., L. A. Bell, and P. Griffin, eds. 1997. *Teaching for Diversity and Social Justice: A Sourcebook.* New York: Routledge.

Apple, M. 1990. *Ideology and Curriculum.* New York: Routledge.

Ashcroft, B., G. Griffiths, and H. Tiffin. 1998. *Key Concepts in Post-Colonial Studies.* London: Routledge.

Austin, G. 1990. *Feminist Theories for Dramatic Criticism.* Ann Arbor: University of Michigan Press.

Bailey, S. D. 1993. *Wings to Fly: Bringing Theatre Arts to Students with Special Needs.* Rockville, MD: Woodbine House.

Banks, J. 1997a. *Educating Citizens in a Multicultural Society.* New York: Teachers College Press.

———. 1997b. "Multicultural Education: Characteristics and Goals." In *Multicultural Education: Issues and Perspectives,* 3d ed., eds. J. Banks and C. McGee Banks, 3–31. Needham Heights, MA: Allyn and Bacon.

———. 1999c. *An Introduction to Multicultural Education.* 2d ed. Needham Heights, MA: Allyn and Bacon.

Banks, J. and C. McGee Banks, eds. 1997. *Multicultural Education: Issues and Perspectives.* Needham Heights, MA: Allyn and Bacon.

Banton, M. 1987. *Racial Theories.* Cambridge: Cambridge University Press.

Quoted in *A Dictionary of Cultural and Critical Theory*, ed. M. Payne (Oxford: Blackwell, 1996), 449.

Beach Center on Families and Disability. 1998. "What You Should Know About Disability." *Beach Center Home Page*. 14 September 1999. <http://www.lsi.ukans.edu/beach/html/y12.htm>.

Beach, M. and L. Pasternack. 1998. "Making a Claim on the Empty Space: An Interview with Terry Galloway." *Theatre Insight* 9 (1): 50–54.

Behar, R. 1996. *The Vulnerable Observer: Anthropology That Breaks Your Heart*. Boston: Beacon Press.

Bem, S. L. 1998. "In a Male-Centered World, Female Differences Are Transformed into Female Disadvantages." In *Race, Class, Gender in the United States*, ed. P. Rothenberg, 48–52. New York: St. Martin's Press.

Berke, R. L. 1998. "The Nation; Chasing The Polls on Gay Rights," *New York Times*, 2 August, sec. 4, p. 3.

Briley, R. 1999. Telephone interview with the author. Tape recording. 10 September.

Brown, B. S. 1998. *Oliver's High Five*. Sante Fe, NM: Health Press.

Bunting, E. 1991. *Fly Away Home*. New York: Clarion.

———. 1994. *Smoky Night*. San Diego, CA: Harcourt Brace.

Butler, J. 1990a. *Gender Trouble*. New York: Routledge.

———. 1990b. "Performative Acts and Gender Constitution." In *Performing Feminisms: Feminist Critical Theory and Theatre*, ed. S. E. Case, 270–282. London: John Hopkins.

Byram, M. and M. Fleming, eds. 1998. *Language Learning in Intercultural Perspective: Approaches Through Drama and Ethnography*. Cambridge, U.K.: Cambridge University Press.

Campbell, D. 1996. *Choosing Democracy: A Practical Guide to Multicultural Education*. Englewood Cliffs, NJ: Prentice Hall.

Campbell, D. and D. D. Campbell. 1996. "How Society and Schools Shortchange Girls and Boys." In *Choosing Democracy: A Practical Guide to Multicultural Education*, ed. D. Campbell, 109–126. Englewood Cliffs, NJ: Prentice Hall.

Campbell, D. and M. Marable. 1996. "Racism and Schools." In *Choosing Democracy: A Practical Guide to Multicultural Education*, ed. D. Campbell, 45–79. Englewood Cliffs, NJ: Prentice Hall.

Casper, V., H. Cuffaro, S. Schultz, J. Silin, and E. Wickens. 1996. "Toward a Most Thorough Understanding of the World: Sexual Orientation and

Early Childhood Education." *Harvard Educational Review* 66(2): 271–293.

Cattanach, A. 1992. *People with Special Needs.* London: A. and C. Black.

Chamberlain, J. 1999. "Bigots Ban Books: Book Banning in Surrey—What Happened?" *EGALE Canada Home Page.* 22 August. <www.egale.ca/features/surrey.htm>.

Chasnoff, D. and H. Cohen, dir. 1997. *It's Elementary: Talking about Gay Issues in School.* Videocassette. Prod. Women's Educational Media.

Childers, J. and G. Hentzi, eds. 1995. *The Columbia Dictionary of Modern Literary and Cultural Criticism.* New York: Columbia University Press.

Consortium of National Arts Education Associations. 1994. *National Standards for Arts Education: What Every Young American Should Know and Be Able to Do in the Arts.* Reston, VA: Music Educators National Conference.

Davis, L. 1995. *Enforcing Normalcy: Disability, Deafness, and the Body.* London: Verso.

———, ed. 1997. "Constructing Normalcy: The Bell Curve, the Novel, and the Invention of the Disabled Body in the Nineteenth Century." In *The Disability Studies Reader,* ed. L. Davis, 9–28. New York: Routledge.

de Beauvoir, S. 1953. *The Second Sex.* New York: Alfred Knopf.

Delpit, L. 1995. *Other People's Children: Cultural Conflict in the Classroom.* New York: The New Press.

Derman-Sparks, L. and ABC Task Force. 1989. *Anti-bias Curriculum Tools for Empowering Young Children.* Washington, D.C.: National Association for the Education of Young Children.

Diaz-Rico, L. 1998. "Towards a Just Society: Recalibrating Multicultural Teachers." In *Speaking the Unpleasant: The Politics of (non)Engagement in the Multicultural Education Terrain,* eds. R. Chavez Chavez and J. O'Donnell, 69–86. Albany, NY: State University of New York.

Dillard, C. 1996. "This Issue." *Theory into Practice.* 35 (4): 230–31.

Du Bois, W. E. B. 1995. *The Souls of Black Folk.* New York: Signet Classic.

Eagleton, T. 1983. *Literary Theory: An Introduction.* Minneapolis: University of Minnesota Press.

———. 1990. *The Significance of Theory.* Oxford: Blackwell.

Ellis, A. and M. Llewellyn. 1997. *Dealing with Differences: Taking Action on Class, Race, Gender, and Disability.* Thousand Oaks, CA: Corwin Press.

Elwin, R. and M. Paulse. 1990. *Asha's Mums.* Toronto: Women's Press.

Ellsworth, E. 1989. "Why Doesn't This Feel Empowering? Working Through the Repressive Myths of Critical Pedagogy." *Harvard Educational Review* 59 (August): 297–324.

"Employment Non-Discrimination Act (ENDA), The." 1999. *Human Rights Campaign Home Page.* 19 October 1999 <http://www.hrc.org/issues/leg/enda/index.html>.

Fiske, S. T. 1993. "Controlling Other People: The Impact of Power on Stereotyping." *American Psychologist* (June): 621–628.

Fletcher, H. 1995. "Retrieving the Mother/Other from the Myths and Margins of O'Neill's 'Seal Wife' Drama." *NADIE Journal* 19 (2): 25–38.

Fringe Benefits Theatre Company. 2000. *Cootie Shots.* New York: Theatre Communications Group (forthcoming).

Fuller, M. L. 1996. "Multicultural Concerns and Classroom Management." In *Making Schooling Multicultural: Campus and Classroom,* eds. C. Grant and M. Gomez, 133–160. Englewood Cliffs, NJ: Prentice Hall.

Garcia, L. 1997. "Drama, Theatre, and the Infusion of Multiethnic Content: An Exploratory Study." *Youth Theatre Journal* 11: 88–101.

———. 1998. "Creating Community in a University Production of *Bocon!*" *Research in Drama Education* 3 (2): 155–166.

———. 1999a. E-mail to the author. 2 October.

———. 1999b. "The Teacher as Cultural Mediator in the Drama Classroom." Paper presented at American Alliance of Theatre and Education Annual Conference, 29 July, in Chicago, IL.

Gay, G. 1977. "Curriculum for Multicultural Teacher Education." In *Pluralism and the American Teacher,* eds. F. H. Klassen and D. M. Gollnick, 31–62. Washington, D.C.: AACTE, Ethnic Heritage Center for Teacher Education.

———. 1997. "Ethnic Minorities and Educational Equality." In *Multicultural Education: Issues and Perspectives,* 3d ed., eds. J. Banks and C. M. Banks, 213. (Needham Heights, MA: Allyn and Bacon, 1993).

Geertz, C. 1973. *The Interpretation of Cultures.* New York: Basic Books.

———. 1986. "The Uses of Diversity." In *Tanner Lectures on Social Values,* vol. 7, ed. S. McMurrin, 253–275. Cambridge, U.K.: Cambridge University Press.

Gender Gaps: Where Schools Still Fail Our Children. 1999. Commissioned by the American Association of University Women Educational Foundation. New York: Marlowe and Company.

Gilmore, P. and D. Martin Smith. 1982. "A Retrospective Discussion of the State of the Art in Ethnography in Education." In *Children In and Out of School*, eds. P. Gilmore and A. Glatthorn, 3–18. Washington, D.C.: Center for Applied Linguistics.

Gilroy, P. 1997. "Scales and Eyes: 'Race' Making Difference." In *Eight Technologies of Otherness*, ed. S. Golding, 190–196. London: Routledge.

Giroux, H. 1992. *Border Crossings*. New York: Routledge.

Goldberg, M. 1974. *Children's Theatre: A Philosophy and a Method*. Englewood Cliffs, NJ: Prentice Hall.

Gollnick, D. and P. Chin. 1994. *Multicultural Education in a Pluralistic Society*. 4th ed. New York: Macmillan.

Gollnick, D. and P. Chin. 1998. *Multicultural Education in a Pluralistic Society*. 5th ed. Upper Saddle River, NJ: Merrill.

Gonzalez, J. B. 1995. "Problematizing the Inclusion of Marginalized Cultures in Aurand Harris's *Yankee Doodle*." *Youth Theatre Journal* 9: 97–108.

Goodman, D. and S. Schapiro. 1997. "Sexism Curriculum Design." In *Teaching for Diversity and Social Justice*, eds. M. Adams, L. Bell, P. Griffin, 110–140. London: Routledge.

Grady, S. 1990. "Cross-Cultural Translation: Considerations for the Use of Creative Drama as an Educational Tool in Kerala, South India." Master's thesis, University of Wisconsin.

———. 1992. "The Postmodern Challenge: Universal Truths Need Not Apply." *Theatre* 23 (2): 15–20.

———. 1996. "Toward the Practice of Theory in Practice." In *Researching Drama and Arts Education: Paradigms and Possibilities*, ed. P. Taylor, 59–71. London: Falmer.

Gramsci, A. 1971. *Selections from the Prison Notebooks*, ed. andtranslated by Q. Hoare and G. Nowell Smith. London: Lawrence and Wishart.

Griffin, P. 1997. "Introductory Module for the Single Issue Courses." In *Teaching for Diversity and Social Justice*, eds. M. Adams, L. A. Bell, and P. Griffin, 61–81. New York: Routledge.

Grummet, M. 1988. *Bitter Milk: Women and Teaching*. Amherst, MA: University of Massachusetts Press.

Halpern, S. 1988. "Portrait of the Artist." Review of *Under the Eye of the Clock* by Christopher Nolan. *New York Time's Review of Books*, June 30: 3–4.

Harbeck, K., ed. 1992a. *Coming Out of the Classroom Closet: Gay and Lesbian Students, Teachers and Curricula*. Binghamton, NY: Harrington Park Press.

Harbeck, K. 1992b. "Gay and Lesbian Educators: Past History/Future Prospects." In *Coming Out of the Classroom Closet,* ed. K. Harbeck, 121–140. Binghamton, NY: Harrington Park Press.

Harrington, M. 1962. *The Other America.* New York: Macmillan.

"Hate Crimes Bill Falls Victim to GOP Leadership." 1999. Press Release 18 October *Human Rights Campaign Home Page.* 18 October <http://www.hrc.org/hrc/hrcnews/1999/991018.html>.

Heinig, R. 1992. *Improvisation with Favorite Tales.* Portsmouth, NH: Heinemann.

Helms, J. 1992. *A Race Is a Nice Thing to Have: A Guide to Being a White Person or Understanding the White Persons in Your Life.* Topeka, KS: Content Communications.

Herik, G. 1989. "The social psychology of homophobia: Toward a practical theory." *Review of Law and Social Change* 14 (4): 923–934. Quoted in B. Cody Murphy, "Educating Mental Health Professionals About Gay and Lesbian Issues," in *Coming Out of the Classroom Closet,* ed. K. Harbeck, 230. Binghamton, NY: Harrington Park Press.

Heward, W. L. 1996. *Exceptional Children: An Introduction to Special Education.* 5th ed. Englewood Cliffs, NJ: Prentice Hall.

Heward, W. L. and R. A. Cavanaugh. 1997. "Educational Equality for Students with Disabilities." In *Multicultural Education: Issues and Perspectives,* 3d ed., ed. J. Banks and C. McGee Banks, 301–333. Needham Heights, MA: Allyn and Bacon.

Hirsch, E. D. 1987. *Cultural Literacy: What Every American Needs to Know.* Boston: Houghton Miflin.

"Homophobia." 1999. *Ontario Consultants on Religious Tolerance Home Page.* 14 August. <http://www.religioustolerance.org/hom_fuel.htm>.

hooks, b. 1990. *Yearning: Race, Gender, and Cultural Politics.* Boston, South End Press.

———. 1994. *Teaching to Transgress.* New York: Routledge.

Hornbrook, D. 1992. "'Can we do ours, Miss?' Towards a Dramatic Curriculum." *The Drama/Theatre Teacher* 4 (2): 16–20.

———. 1998. *Education and Dramatic Art.* 2d ed. London: Routledge.

Hostile Hallways: The AAUW Survey on Sexual Harassment in America's Schools. 1993. Washington, D.C.: American Association of University Women Educational Foundation.

How Schools Shortchange Girls: The AAUW Report, a Study of Major Findings on Girls and Education. 1992. Researched by the Wellesley College Center for Research on Women. Washington, D.C.: American Association of University Women Educational Foundation.

Howard, G. 1999. *We Can't Teach What We Don't Know.* New York: Teachers College Press.

Hubbard, R. 1998. "Rethinking Women's Biology." In *Race, Class, Gender in the United States,* ed. P. Rothenberg, 32–33. New York: St. Martin's Press.

Hundley, K. 1998. "Board: Keep books: 'Heather Has Two Mommies' may be moved to juvenile or adult section, while 'Daddy's Roommate' is deemed appropriate for the children's section of the library." 24 June. *Times Record News Online.* 20 August 1999. <http://www.wtr.com/text_only_html/6_24_98.htm>.

Jacobson, M. F. 1998. *Whiteness of a Different Color: European Immigrants and the Alchemy of Race.* Cambridge, MA: Harvard University Press.

Jehlen, M. 1995. "Gender." In *Critical Terms for Literary Study,* ed. F. Lentricchia and T. McLaughlin, 263–273. Chicago: University of Chicago Press.

Jones, J. 1972. *Prejudice and Racism.* Reading, MA: Addison Wesley. Quoted in J. Helms, *A Race Is a Nice Thing to Have: A Guide to Being a White Person or Understanding the White Persons in Your Life* (Topeka, KS: Content Communications, 1992), 17.

Joyce, G. 1998. "Court overturns school board ban on same-sex books." *Canadian Press,* 16 December. Quoted on *EGALE Home Page.* 22 August 1999. <http://www.egale.ca/archives/press/9812cp.htm>.

Kadi, J. 1996. *Thinking Class: Sketches from a Cultural Worker.* Boston: South End Press.

Katz, K. 1999. *The Colors of Us.* New York: Henry Holt.

Kemp, A., ed. 1996. *Drama Education and Special Needs.* Cheltenham, U.K.: Stanley Thornes.

Kentucky Center for the Arts. N.D. "Appendix C: Guide to Etiquette and Behavior for Working With Persons with Disabilities."

King, J. L. 1991. "Dysconscious Racism: Ideology, Identity, and the Miseducation of Teachers." *Journal of Negro Education* 60(2):133–146.

King, J. L., E. Hollins, and W. Hayman, eds. 1997. *Preparing Teachers for Cultural Diversity.* New York: Teachers College Press.

Kozol, J. 1991. *Savage Inequalities: Children in America's Schools.* New York: Crown Publishers.

Kristeva, J. 1991. *Strangers to Ourselves.* Translated by L. S. Roudiez. New York: Columbia University Press.

Ladson-Billings, G. 1994. *The Dreamkeepers: Successful Teachers of African American Children.* San Francisco: Jossey-Bass Publishers.

Lakoff, G. and M. Johnson. 1980. *Metaphors We Live By.* Chicago, IL: University of Chicago Press.

"Lesson of Matthew Shepard, The." 1998. *New York Times,* 17 October, sec. A, p. 14.

Libman, K. 1998. "Embracing Her Body: Sexuality and Female Adolescent Characters in Three Plays for Young Audiences." *Youth Theatre Journal,* 12:48–59.

Lincoln, Y. and E. Guba. 1985. *Naturalistic Inquiry.* Newbury Park, CA: Sage.

Manley, A. and C. O'Neill. 1997. *Dreamseekers: Creative Approaches to the African American Heritage.* Portsmouth, NH: Heinemann.

Mantsios, G. 1998. "Class in America: Myths and Realities." In *Race, Class, Gender in the United States: An Integrated Study,* ed. P. Rothenberg, 202–214. New York: St. Martin's Press.

Masud-Piloto, F. 1995. "Nuestra Realidad: Historical Roots of Our Latino Identity." In *Beyond Comfort Zones in Multiculturalism: Confronting the Politics of Privilege,* eds. S. Jackson and J. Solís, 53–63. Westport, CT: Bergin and Garvey.

McGrath, J. 1981. *A Good Night Out.* London: Eyre Methuen.

McIntyre, A. 1997. *Making Meaning of Whiteness: Exploring Racial Identity with White Teachers.* Albany, NY: State University of New York Press.

McLaren, P. 1994. "Multiculturalism and the Postmodern Critique: Toward a Pedagogy of Resistance and Transformation." In *Between Borders: Pedagogy and the Politics of Cultural Studies,* eds. H. Giroux and P. McLaren, 192–222. New York: Routledge.

Minh-ha, T. T. 1986–7. "Introduction." *Discourse* 8 (Fall / Winter): 1–9.

Mirus, G. 1999. E-mail to the author. 26 August.

Moi, T. 1986. "Feminist Literary Criticism" In *Modern Literary Theory: A Comparative Introduction,* 2d ed., eds. A. Jefferson and D. Robey, 204. London: Batsford. Quoted in J. Hawthorn, *A Concise Glossary of Contemporary Literary Theory* (London: Hodder and Stoughton, 1992), 62.

Morgan, N. and J. Saxton. 1987. *Teaching Drama: A Mind of Many Wonders.* London: Hutchinson.

Moore, Henrietta. 1990. *Feminism and Anthropology.* Minneapolis: University of Minnesota Press, 7. Quoted in D. Gollnick and P. Chin, *Multicultural Education in a Pluralistic Society.* 5th ed. (Upper Saddle River, NJ: Merrill, 1998), 122.

Munsch, R. 1980. *The Paper Bag Princess.* Toronto: Annick Press.

Murphy, B. C. 1992. "Educating Mental Health Professionals About Gay and Lesbian Issues." In *Coming Out of the Classroom Closet,* ed. K. Harbeck, 229–246. Binghamton, NY: Harrington Park Press.

National Endowment for the Arts. 1994. "Guidance on How to Write and Speak About People with Disabilities and Older Adults." Duplicated memo.

Nicholson, H. 1995. "Performative Acts: Drama, Education and Gender." *NADIE Journal* 19 (1): 27–38.

———. 1993. "Postmodernism and Educational Drama." *Drama* 2 (1): 18–21.

Nieto, S. 1992. *Affirming Diversity: The Sociopolitical Context of Multicultural Education.* White Plains, NY: Longman.

Nutting, D. 1999. Interview by the author. Tape recording. Austin, Texas. 16 September.

O'Hara, E. and C. Lanoux. 1998. "Deconstructing Barbie." Session presentation at American Alliance of Theatre and Education Annual Conference, August, in Denver, CO.

———. 1999. "Deconstructing Barbie: Using Creative Drama as a Tool for Image Making in Pre-Adolescent Girls." *STAGE of the Art* 10 (3): 8–13.

Omi, M. and H. Winant. 1994. *Racial Formation in the United States.* New York: Routledge.

O'Neill, C. 1995. *Drama Worlds: A Framework for Process Drama.* Portsmouth, NH: Heinemann.

Oram, H. 1992. *Reckless Ruby.* London: Picture Lions.

Orenstein, P. 1994. *School Girls: Young Women, Self-Esteem, and the Confidence Gap.* New York: Doubleday.

Pallas, A. M., G. Natriello, and E. L. McDill. 1989. "The Changing Nature of the Disadvantaged Population: Current Dimensions and Future Trends." *Educational Researcher* 18 (5): 16–22.

Payne, R. 1995. *Poverty: A Framework for Understanding and Working with Students and Adults from Poverty.* Baytown, TX: RFT Publishers.

Pearson-Davis, S. 1993. "Cultural Diversity in Children's Theatre and Creative Drama." *Youth Theatre Journal* 7 (4): 3–18.

———. 1999. E-mail to the author. 1 November.

Peter, M. 1995. *Making Drama Special: Developing Drama Practice to Meet Special Educational Needs.* London: David Fulton.

Pearce, M. 1996. "Inclusion: Twelve Secrets to Making it Work in Your Classroom." *Instructor* 106 (2) :81–85.

Pipher, M. 1994. *Reviving Ophelia: Saving the Selves of Adolescent Girls.* New York: Ballantine.

Polacco, P. 1998. *Thank You, Mr. Falker.* New York: Philomel Books.

Pollack, W. 1998. *Real Boys: Rescuing Our Sons from the Myth of Boyhood.* New York: Henry Holt and Company.

Quin, L. 1998. "Some residents angry over book flap: Wichitans object to ministers' stance against books about children with homosexual parents, vow to donate more books." 19 May. *Times Record News Online.* 20 August 1999. <http://www.wtr.com/html/5_19_98_some_residents_angry_over_book_flap.htm>.

Riherd, M. and N. Swortzell. 1996. "Multiculturalism and Educational Theatre." In *Making Schooling Multicultural: Campus and Classroom,* eds. C. Grant and M. Gomez, 327–48. Englewood Cliffs, NJ: Merrill.

Robles de Meléndez, W. and V. Ostertag. 1997. *Teaching Young Children in Multicultural Classrooms: Issues, Concepts, and Strategies.* Albany, NY: Delmar.

Rofes, E. 1997a. "Gay Issues, Schools, and the Right-wing Backlash." *Rethinking Schools Online.* 14 August 99. <http:www//rethinkingschools.org/Archives/11_03/rofes.htm>.

Rofes, E. 1997b. "Schools: The Neglected Site of Queer Activists." Foreword to *School Experiences of Gay and Lesbian Youth: The Invisible Minority* ed. M. B. Harris, xiii–xviii. New York: Haworth.

Rose, P. 1997. *They and We: Racial and Ethnic Relations in the United States.* 5th ed. New York: McGraw-Hill.

Rothenberg, P., ed. 1998. "Part I: The Social Construction of Difference: Race, Class, Gender and Sexuality." In *Race, Class, Gender in the United States: An Integrated Study,* 7–12. New York: St. Martin's Press.

Sadker, M. and D. Sadker. 1986. *PEPA (Principal Effectiveness, Pupil Achievement): A Training Program for Principals and Other Educational Leaders.* Washington, D.C.: American University. Quoted in M. Sadker, D. Sadker, and L. Long, "Gender and Educational Equity," in *Multicultural Education: Issues and Perspectives,* 3d ed., ed. J. Banks and C. McGee Banks, 145–146. Needham Heights, MA: Allyn and Bacon.

———. 1994. *Failing at Fairness: How Our Schools Cheat Girls.* New York: Simon and Schuster.

Sadker, M., D. Sadker, and S. Klein. 1991. "The Issue of Gender in Elementary and Secondary Education." In *Review of Research in Education,* ed. G. Grant, 309. Washington: American Educational Research Association. Quoted in D. Gollnick and P. Chin, *Multicultural Education in a Pluralistic Society,* 4th ed. (New York: Macmillan, 1994).

Sadker, M., D. Sadker, and L. Long. 1997. "Gender and Educational Equality." In *Multicultural Education: Issues and Perspectives,* 3d ed., ed. J. Banks and C. McGee Banks, 131–149. Needham Heights, MA: Allyn and Bacon.

Salat, C. 1999. *Living in Secret.* Orinda, CA: Books MareUs.

Saldaña, J. 1991. "Drama, Theatre, and Hispanic Youth: Interviews with Selected Teachers and Artists." *Youth Theatre Journal* 5 (4):3–8.

———. 1995. *Drama of Color: Improvisation with Multiethnic Folklore.* Portsmouth, NH: Heinemann.

———. 1999a. "Improvisation with the '-Isms': Racism—'Playground Politics.'" *Multicultural and Diversity Committee Spring Newsletter* 5 (2): 3–4.

———. 1999b. "Social Class and Social Consciousness: Adolescent Perception of Oppression in Forum Theatre Workshops." *Multicultural Perspectives.* 1 (3): 14–18

Sears, J. 1992. "Educators, Homosexuality, and Homosexual Students: Are Personal Feelings Related to Professional Beliefs?" In *Coming Out of the Classroom Closet,* ed. K. Harbeck, 29–80. Binghamton, NY: Harrington Park Press.

Shapiro, J. 1993. *No Pity: People with Disabilities Forging a New Civil Rights Movements.* New York: Times Books. Quoted in Ellis, A. and M. Llewellyn, *Dealing with Differences: Taking Action on Class, Race, Gender, and Disability* (Thousand Oaks, CA: Corwin Press, 1997), 110–112.

Shortchanging Girls, Shortchanging America: Executive Summary. 1991. Washington, D.C.: American Association of University Women.

Sleeter, C. 1996. *Multicultural Education as Social Activism.* Albany: State University of New York Press.

Sleeter, C. and C. Grant. 1994. *Making Choices for Multicultural Education: Five Approaches to Race, Class, and Gender.* 2d ed. New York: Macmillan.

———. 1998. *Turning on Learning: Five Approaches for Multicultural Teaching Plans for Race, Class, Gender, and Disability.* 2d ed. Upper Saddle River, NJ: Merrill.

Spivak, G. 1990. *The Post-colonial Critic: Interviews, Strategies, Dialogues.* New York: Routledge.

Tatum, B. D. 1999. *"Why Are All the Black Kids Sitting Together in the Cafeteria?" and Other Conversations About Race.* New York: Basic Books.

Tuite, P. 1998. "Assimilating Immigrants Through Drama: The Social Politics of Alice Minnie Herts and Lillian Wald." *Youth Theatre Journal* 12: 10–18.

"Unacceptable!" 1997. Editorial. *Augusta Chronicle Online.* 17 September. 14 August 99 <http://www.augustachronicle.com/stories/091797/nea.html>.

Uribe, V. and K. Harbeck. 1992. "Addressing the Needs of Lesbian, Gay, and Bisexual Youth: The Origins of PROJECT 10 and School-based Intervention." In *Coming Out of the Classroom Closet,* ed. K. Harbeck, 9–28. Binghamton, NY: Harrington Park Press.

U.S. Bureau of the Census. 1990. "Disability: 1990 Census Table 3." *U.S. Census Bureau Home Page.* 15 September 1999. <http://www.census.gov/hhes/www/disable/census/tables/tab3us.html>.

U.S. Bureau of the Census. 1994. "Statistical Brief 94–1: Americans with Disabilities." *U.S. Census Bureau Home Page.* 15 September 1999. <http://www.census.gov/apsd/www/statbrief/sb94_1.pdf>.

U.S. Bureau of the Census. 1997. "Disabilities affect one-fifth of all Americans." *U.S. Census Bureau Home Page.* 15 September 1999. <http://www.census.gov/hhes/www/disable.html>.

Wagner, B. J. 1998. *Educational Drama and Language Arts: What Research Shows.* Portsmouth, NH: Heinemann.

Webster's Ninth New Collegiate Dictionary. 1990. Springfield, MA: Merriam-Webster.

Wellman, D. 1977. *Portraits of White Racism.* Cambridge, U.K.: Cambridge University Press. Quoted in B. D. Tatum, *"Why Are All the Black Kids Sitting Together in the Cafeteria?" and Other Conversations About Race* (New York: Basic Books, 1999), 7.

Wendell, S. 1996. *The Rejected Body: Feminist Philosophical Reflections on Disability.* New York: Routledge.

———. 1997. "Toward a Feminist Theory of Disability." In *The Disability Studies Reader,* ed. L. Davis, 260–278. New York: Routledge.

Wijeyesinghe, C. L., P. Griffin, and B. Love. 1997. "Racism Curriculum Design." In *Teaching for Diversity and Social Justice*, eds. M. Adams, L. A. Bell, and P. Griffin, 82–109. New York: Routledge.

Winston, J. 1998. *Drama, Narrative and Moral Education.* London: Falmer.

Winston, J. and M. Tandy. 1998. *Beginning Drama 4–11.* London: David Fulton.

Winterson, J. 1989. *Sexing the Cherry.* London: Vintage.

Wolfson, M. 1998. "Books under fire: Religious leaders denounce gay stories." 16 May. *Times Record News Online.* 20 August 1999 <http://www.wtr.com/html/5_16_98.htm>.

Wood, A. 1985. *King Bidgood's in the Bathtub.* San Diego, CA: Harcourt Brace.

Wood, D. 1992. *The Power of Maps.* New York: Guildford Press.

Woods, S. E. and K. Harbeck. 1992. "Living in Two Worlds: The Identity Management Strategies Used by Lesbian Physical Educators." In *Coming Out of the Classroom Closet*, ed. K. Harbeck, 141–166. Binghamton, NY: Harrington Park Press.

Woodson, S. E. 1998. "Underlying Constructs in the Development and Institutionalization of the Child Drama Field." *Youth Theatre Journal* 12: 1–9.

Woodward, J. 1972. "Implications for Sociolinguistics Research Among the Deaf." *Sign Language Studies* 1: 1–7.

Zollo, C. 1998. "Jeffress vows to continue fight." 29 June. *Times Record News Online.* 20 August 1999. <http://www.wtr.com/text_only_html/6_29_98.htm>

Index